2nd Edition REVISED!

THE
COSTA RICA
TRAVELER

Getting Around
In Costa Rica

By Ellen Searby

Windham Bay Press
Occidental, California

First edition January 1985
Second edition January 1988
  Fifth printing, updated, March 1990

Also published by Windham Bay Press:

Alaska's Inside Passage Traveler, See More/Spend Less! by Ellen Searby

The Vancouver Island Traveler, Great Adventures on Canada's West Rim by Sandy Bryson

Front Cover: Rare Resplendent Quetzal (photo by Michael Fogden).

Back Cover: A Beach Waiting for You, near Marenco on the Osa Peninsula.

Black and white photos by Ellen Searby and Sandy Bryson. Maps by Ellen Searby.

Windham Bay Press
Box 1198, Occidental, CA 95465

FOREWORD

Costa Rica has more choices of things to see and do with less distance between them than any other place I've been. In the space of 75 miles across its narrowest width, the land goes from sea level to over 12,000 feet and back to sea level. There are many landscapes and climates between, and the wide variety of plants and animals they support. Costa Rica would offer fine traveling and vacations even if this were all.

"We have so much to share," is a slogan of Costa Rica's tourism department, the Instituto Costarricense de Turismo (ICT). Costa Rica has 2½ million of the most friendly, helpful people in the world. A Canadian visitor wrote, "They treat you with a quiet dignity, like a guest in their home, instead of an invading tourist." Their pride in their country, its freedom and literacy, and their willingness to share it with the traveler, are a joy—and a lesson in humanity.

Before I vacationed in Costa Rica the first time, a U.S. friend described it as "the most hassle-free foreign travel you'll ever do." Even with almost no Spanish, except numbers, I found she was right. People helped any time they could think of a way to do so. They've met enough travelers to know what we want and have kept their considerate nature without becoming cynical. Meeting the Costa Ricans is as much a privilege as traveling in the beauty of their country.

OUR SECOND EDITION

In the 3 years since *The Costa Rica Traveler* was first published, there have been many changes in Costa Rica. What has **not** changed is the friendly hospitality of the people and peace in the country. Costa Ricans have worked persistently for peace in Central America. President Arias received the 1987 Nobel Peace Prize for his peace plan and efforts to bring peace with justice to the region.

Meanwhile tourist facilities, roads, and tours, especially for nature-lovers, have increased. We inspected 200 hotels and cabinas for this edition, some of them just opened. Many of you have written or told me your experiences with tourist services and asked for additional information in this next edition. With no paid advertising in this book, I have felt free to comment on facilities as we found them. While Costa Rica is a real place in the real world of developing countries, everyone I have met has enjoyed his trip and many have returned for another visit.

ACKNOWLEDGMENTS

I owe thanks to many people who helped me gather and update information for this edition. Without them I couldn't have done it.

Special thanks to LACSA, Costa Rica' s airline. They helped me with this project, and their promotion has helped tourism in Costa Rica greatly. Sr. Jose Giralt and Sra. Maria Amalia Marti took time from very busy schedules to help me and this book.

Within the Instituto Costarricense de Turismo (known in Costa Rica as ICT and in the U.S. as the Costa Rican Tourist Board), the following people answered all the questions I could ask—or found someone who could: Edgar Bailey, Robert Chaverri, Elmo Delanoce, Roberto Morales, and drivers Jorge Chacon and Rodrigo Herrera who drove and guided us on many miles of back roads.

Michael Kaye and Jim Lewis of Costa Rica Expeditions and their staff and Archie Fields of Rio Colorado Lodge offered suggestions, answered many questions, and provided transportation when we had no time to wait for buses or public boats. Lee Weiler at the Hotel Don Carlos and Richard Dyer and Jerry Ruhlow at the *Tico Times* gave information and useful advice. Mr. and Mrs. Pablo Hurtado were incredibly helpful and hospitable.

Any errors in the book are my responsibility, not theirs. Their explanation of their country and their culture was wonderful. May you enjoy it as much as I do!

Sandy Bryson, writer, photographer and an old friend, shared the work of hotel inspection throughout Costa Rica and took many excellent photos, some of them in this edition.

Henry Jori, my husband, edited and proofread copy, offered many useful suggestions, and gave moral support and encouragement while I worked on this project.

TABLE OF CONTENTS

5

The National Theater in San Jose, Costa Rica's architectural treasure.

COSTA RICA

If there is a tropical Camelot, peaceful Costa Rica is it. Despite military and political turbulence in its neighbors, Costa Rica has the best working democracy in Latin America, the freest, most honest elections, and the highest literacy rate in the region. Beset with the same economic, social, and environmental problems that face other developing nations, Costa Rica is much farther along the road to solution than most others.

Costa Rica is tiny, about the size of West Virginia. You can fly into San Jose, the capital, up in the Central Valley, and decide whether you want to swim in the Atlantic or Pacific that afternoon!

WHY COME? MAJOR ATTRACTIONS

Costa Rica in its small space has many attractions that are major by any standard. Among them are:

Conchal, a sheltered white sand beach in Guanacaste.

Beaches

Costa Rica has hundreds of beaches, almost all uncrowded. You may find yourself the only person on a beach five miles long! Do you prefer white, black, yellow, or red sand? Costa Rica has them all. Do you want to surf, snorkel, walk on a wild driftwood-littered beach, watch thousands of sea turtles come ashore to lay eggs in the sand, watch baby turtles freshly hatched crawl down to the sea, swim or wade in calm water, gather agates and moonstones polished by waves, fish for tarpon, marlin, and other gamefish, walk palm-shaded paths along the shore watching for parrots, monkeys, egrets, and end the day enjoying one of the world's finest sunsets?

All Costa Rican beaches seem to have at least four or five of the above features. You can pick an area suited to your interests. Usually several nearby beaches have different attractions, which add variety to your vacation.

Do take seriously local advice on rip currents which exist at most beaches with surf. If you are caught in a current that carries you out, don't exhaust yourself fighting it, but swim

8

parallel to the shore until you are free and then swim back in. Note that you may need to be able to swim for up to an hour— and don't swim in such places unless you can. Study diagrams posted that show you how to recognize and avoid rip currents. Beaches which always deserve respect for rips include Junquillal, Jacó, Esterillos, and First Beach at Manuel Antonio. Costa Rica has many beaches that a two year-old can safely splash on anytime.

Accommodations vary from some of the world's finest hotels, through very comfortable, reasonably priced cabins and motels, to basic cabinas and rooms, and, of course, camping out. These are described individually in their regions later in this book.

Third Beach at Manuel Antonio.

Poas crater.

Volcanoes

Costa Rica's backbone north and east of San Jose is a chain of volcanoes extending down from Mexico through Central America. Costa Rica has 10, 3 of them active. You can ride public buses or bus tours from San Jose to the tops of Irazú, 11,260 ft., and Poás, 9,500 ft. Others are reached by hiking, horse, or jeep trail. Irazú erupted in 1963, showering San Jose with 5 inches of ash, causing millions of colones in damage to property, livestock, and the 1964 coffee crop, but enriching the Central Valley soil for years to come. On a clear morning you can see both the Atlantic and Pacific Oceans from its summit.

Poás last erupted in 1978, but has a constantly varying steam cloud boiling up from the fumaroles in its crater. Both volcanoes have overlooks at the edge of their craters with fantastic views of the banded rocks and ash that form their rims. Riding up these heights, you pass from warm to a very cool and cloudy tropical climate. Coffee plantations give way to dairy cattle and potato patches on terraces up the steep slopes. In the cloud forests at higher elevations, tree branches support communities of bromeliads, orchids, and other plants. Up here in the clouds, the forest and the ash-covered slopes near the craters are another world from the busy streets of San Jose.

White-faced or capuchin monkeys at Manuel Antonio.

National Parks

Costa Rica has done an incredible thing for any nation, much less a struggling developing country—it has set aside 11% of its small space in a national park system, one of the world's most important. As tropical forests are cut everywhere, these preserved areas are the only hope of saving many plant and animal species. There is at least one sample of every ecosystem in the country within the park system.

All the volcanic summits are within parks or biological preserves. Santa Rosa is a dry tropical forest, while Corcovado in the southwest is a rolling, wet lowland with as many bird species as the United States and Canada combined. Some parks preserve cultural or archeological features, such as prehistoric village sites.

There's something for most travelers in the parks. You can watch sea turtles come ashore to lay their eggs in the sand at Tortuguero and Santa Rosa and come back several months later to see newly hatched babies scramble down to the sea. At Caño Island and Cahuita you can snorkel on coral reefs. At Rincon de la Vieja you can walk up to thermal springs and "pailes," springs of boiling mud. In Santa Rosa's dry forest, undergrowth and vines are widely spaced and you have clear views of monkeys, coatimundis, peccaries, armadillos, and hundreds of birds. I saw all of these on one walk there.

Costa Rica's limited park budget is going to the preservation of these precious habitats for wildlife, while most unprotected land is being cut over for lumber and to make cattle range. Funds aren't being spent for building plush facilities or even access roads in some cases. While you can drive up to some parks by bus, La Amistad, the newest and largest, covering the Talamanca Range along the Panamanian border, may only be reached by dirt roads to the park boundaries on both east and west sides. There is not a single lodge or hotel within the parks. For the more remote parks, arrangements must be made with park headquarters in San Jose so the staff knows what help you'll need—space in a bunkroom, use of cooking facilities, guide, possibly horses to rent if the rangers don't need them that day, etc.

If your time is limited and you want to see the maximum wildlife in remote parks, you may want to go on a nature tour led by biologists. Smithsonian, Massachusetts Audubon Society, Mountain Travel, and other adventure tour operators organize these. Within Costa Rica, there are several outfitters whose addresses are given in our Sources of Information section near the end of the book.

Early morning birdwatchers enter Manuel Antonio.

Birds and Wildlife

Costa Rica is home, seasonally, to ¹⁄₁₀th of the world's bird species, over 850 (the U. S. and Canada combined have about 350)! For such a small country, this seems impossible, but Costa Rica's 12,600 feet of altitude range, wet and dry zones, and strategic location in the overlap between North and South American bird ranges account for it. This nation's dedicated protection of those habitats may be all that keeps many of these species alive.

From trips to the zoo, you know that tropical birds are often brighter and more spectacular than most temperate birds, though nearly invisible types of brown twitters (my term which saves reaching for the bird book) are found in every forest. Chattering groups of parrots and lorikeets fly overhead in early morning and evening. An early morning look in any hotel garden or city park is rewarding.

13

Costa Rica's pride is the resplendent quetzal, never found in zoos, but living in the high, cool forests of Monteverde and Chirripó. With its red underside, iridescent green back and trailing green tail plumes, it is like no other! It is most easily seen on guided trips in Monteverde in March and April, when it is nesting and less cautious than usual—and the guide knows where the nests and food trees are. The quetzal's picture on our cover shows why so many visitors come far to see it.

Depending on location, season, and luck, you may see scarlet macaws, tanagers and orioles, toucans, and waterfowl of all kinds including roseate spoonbills and the rare jabiru stork. Estuaries and lagoons where small rivers reach the sea may have a dozen species visible at a time, very near the beach hotel you're staying in. Palo Verde National Park at the mouth of the Tempisque River is a great waterfowl haven that attracts naturalists from many nations.

A biologist from Cornell was studying hummingbirds at Monteverde. Knowing there were several pages of them in my bird book, I asked how many there were in her area. "Thirty species, but only eight common."

When you're watching birds or monkeys in the bush, it's very easy to forget the ground at your feet. Don't. In Rincon de la Vieja National Park, I saw my first Rey de Zopilote (king buzzard) in the wild. It's a huge, creamy-white bird with black on the wings and a red and orange head. I stepped off the horse I'd been riding, camera in hand, and got 4 photos before ants from the hill I was standing on reached and stung my neck! With that lack of care, I was lucky there wasn't a snake.

Guided tours are the easiest way to be sure of seeing certain birds, and may be the only practical way to get to Corcovado National Park, usually reached by charter flight. Recently nature tours have grown in numbers and variety, generally providing tours and guides in the national parks, biological reserves where they are often the only groups permitted, and on some private reserves. Addresses of those operating at press time are given in our Sources of Information section at the back of this book. Particularly if you want a multi-day tour, it's best to write the operators some months in advance and ask which adventure travel and nature tour organizations are sending them groups.

14

Don't Rush Me! Female 3-toed sloth crosses a road, slowly of course, at Manuel Antonio and climbs a tree.

With an expert guide, I watched one group identify over 150 bird species in 4 days, including the quetzal and the three-wattled bell bird.

At press time these people are offering nature tours: **Costa Rica Expeditions** was the first to offer such tours, some with access by white water raft. They run tours to all the important wildlife viewing areas in Costa Rica, often several areas in one tour, including Monteverde. They own Tortuga Lodge which they use as a base for tours in Tortuguero National Park. **Rios Tropicales** offers several tours including one day raft float trips on the quiet Corobici River with iguanas, many varieties of land birds and waterfowl. **Finca Ob-la-di,Ob-la-da** offers horseback tours of a working cattle ranch west of San Jose where forest with birds and monkeys has been preserved. **Horizontes** takes people to Marenco Biological Station, a rustic lodge on the Osa Peninsula just north of Corcovado Park. Besides exploring the beaches and private forest reserve of the station, guests ride boats to Caño Island for snorkeling and hiking and hike inside Corcovado National Park. **Geotur** offers one day tours with a naturalist to Carara Biological Reserve and Braulio Carrillo National Park. **Papagayo Tours**, based at Playa Tamarindo, cruises mangrove channels and turtle nesting beaches. **Rara Avis** has a lodge with its own forest reserve near Braulio Carrillo and La Selva Biological Reserve. Some of their trips feature backpacking. **Selva Verde Lodge**, owned by Holbrook Travel in Florida, is a rustic lodge on a private forest near La Selva. This list does not include several other excellent tours which point out occasional wildlife on the canales or on a general interest tour.

For these trips or for looking on your own, you'll want binoculars, insect repellent, a shade hat, sunscreen, a day pack and canteen, a rain parka, and good walking shoes. Bird books printed outside Costa Rica are very expensive within the country, so it's worth bringing them with you. Roger Tory Peterson's *Birds of Mexico* is very useful and would be more so if he had illustrated all the birds instead of simply referring to ones shown in his books on Eastern, Western, and Texas birds. For at least the southern half of the country, *Birds of Panama*, by Robert Ridgley, is recommended. The pictures in both of these books are enough to bring any avid birder to Costa Rica.

Pacific screech owls choose a safe perch in a pochote tree for midday nap.

Mammals and reptiles in Costa Rica are as diverse as the birds, but generally fewer and much harder to spot. Some are nocturnal and some live only in the tree canopy far above the ground. Many are endangered, due more to loss of habitat than overhunting, except in the case of sea turtles. Jaguars, ocelots, marguays, howler, squirrel, spider and capuchin monkeys, sloths, deer, tapirs, peccaries, agoutis, coatimundis, foxes, coyotes, armadillos, and manatees are among the animals. You can see most of them in the zoo in San Jose. Iguanas and crocodiles are common in some areas. Green turtles nest on the Caribbean coast, primarily at Tortuguero, and leatherback and Pacific Ridley turtles nest on several Pacific beaches.

While many of these animals are not only shy but nocturnal, an early morning or early evening watch at a water hole, especially in drier Guanacaste, is a good way to see them. I've seen howler monkeys, storks, and deer in streams beside highway bridges (when someone else was driving). Even in national parks where they do exist, many are rarely seen. Good luck.

Strangler fig tree stands over 100 ft tall after killing the tree it originally grew on at Monteverde.

Flora

Costa Rica's flowers, flowering trees and shrubs, and an incredible variety of other tropical plants are a delight to anyone. February and March are the height of the blooming season for trees, including the red Poro tree used for living fence posts along roads.

The national flower is an orchid, and there are nearly 1,200 known species of orchids, with some estimates as high as 2,000, in the country. At all seasons, some varieties are in bloom.

Finding one beside a trail in the Monteverde forest was a thrill I won't forget. Collecting orchids is done only by government permit, and then you probably couldn't get them back into your home country. Bring a close-up lens and collect them on film!

The annual orchid show in San Jose in March has a fantastic variety. Any time of year you can visit the Lankester orchid gardens, now run by the University of Costa Rica, on the road between Cartago and Paraiso, open 9 a.m. to 3 p.m.

Within the national parks and in other areas that haven't been deforested, you can enjoy magnificent tropical hardwood trees with huge trunks and spreading branches, often supporting colonies of bromeliads and other plants on branches and trunks. Even in yards everywhere you may find 6-foot samples of shrubs you struggle to grow in tiny pots at home. From landscaped hotel grounds and urban parks to primeval forests and coconut walks along the Caribbean, the variety and colors are thrilling, with surprises on every walk.

Waterfall in the forest near Playa Montezuma.

Passengers carrying local produce board the train to Limon.

The Train to Puerto Limón

Known as the Northern or Atlantic Railway, this 100-mile narrow-gauge train, completed in 1890, was the key to development of Costa Rica. Until it was built, the country's only export, coffee, had to be hauled by oxcart and pack mule down mountain trails to Puntarenas on the west coast and around Cape Horn by ship to market.

Today the ride from San Jose to Puerto Limón (or the reverse, which takes an additional 2 hours because of the climb) is an unforgettable tour of Costa Rican life and country. You can join a tour run by Swiss Travel which includes a guide, semi-private car, lunch and refreshments, leaving the train at Siquirres to return via a visit to a banana plantation to San Jose in one day. Or you can simply buy a ticket to Limón at the train station at Avenida 3, Calle 21, and climb aboard. Get the current schedule from ICT or the station.

Schedules change, but when I rode, the choice was between the noon "express" run that only made 7 stops and the morning

20

52-stop "local," both of which arrived at about the same time. I chose the morning, noting that the train would stay still 52 times while I took pictures. More recently, the only train has left San Jose at 11 a.m., covering the last part ot the trip and arriving in a rough district of Puerto Limón in the dark. Some Costa Ricans prefer to ride the train up from Limón, starting in the cool of the morning, climbing as the day gets warmer, so you arrive about midday in San Jose. Your ticket is a long strip with all the stops printed on it! Try to get a seat on the right side if you're riding to Limón as that's where the best views are until late afternoon. If you're traveling on your own,

From the train you have fine views into the Gorge of the Rio Reventazon.

you'll want to bring some food for the 6-hour ride, along with lots of film. Recently, 3 cars, a locomotive and a dining car have been renovated in 1930s style. There may be an additional charge, but the comfort is worth it.

If you don't want to stay overnight, you could ride a bus back in just over 2 hours, but late at night. The best trip under current schedules is riding up from Limón or riding down from San Jose to Siquirres and riding a bus back.

This isn't a ride simply to get to the coast. Since the highway was built, the fastest, cheapest way is by bus, but if you go on your own, the train is an awful lot of entertainment for about $2!

The train starts with a whistle and jolts, rattling along through the eastern suburbs of San Jose, between banks covered with blooming red impatiens. You look over plastered walls into backyards as children peer back. After several stops, the train climbs the grade past the national oil storage tanks and drops down into Cartago for a longer stop. More people get on and you continue between the slopes of coffee. At villages of only half a dozen houses clinging to the hill, the train stops and children in freshly washed clothes get on to ride down to the town with the nearest school. They ride the afternoon train home. Vendors board selling food and bottled soda. These villages are here only because of the train, and no road goes near many of them. The barest shacks of rusty sheet metal and scrap lumber have pots of flowering plants hanging or lined up on the porch.

When you think of modern office workers commuting on freeways and living in condominiums traveling this far on vacation for a few days compared with these people living in clean air among their ever-blooming plants on the mountainside overlooking a river roaring in the canyon below, you may wonder who's poor.

The 6-car train pulled by a diesel locomotive rattles and sways around turns so tight you often look out and see the rest of the train. The route looks like a mule trail cut across the steep mountain. Now it crosses a gully and you look almost straight down hundreds of feet into the jungle. Across the Reventazón River tall trees of many species, draped with vines Tarzan might use, extend from river to mountain tops. You wonder how many jaguars and monkeys are watching you!

After several hours you read the fading paint of a station sign and look for its name on your ticket. It's only about 2 inches down the long strip! you stand up and stretch while the train sways on.

Looking down a ravine where the rocks supporting the railroad ties are slung in wire nets over space, you aren't surprised that

Vendors sell snacks as the train rattles on.

6,000 people died building the railway, though malaria in the eastern lowlands was the main killer. The young American, Minor Keith, struggled with the project for nearly 20 years before it was done. When some miles of track were laid from the east coast and money was running short, Keith imported banana seedlings and started the plantations that led to United Fruit Company. Jamaican workers were brought in, as they were more resistant than others to malaria, and were given land along the track.

As the train drops down eastern slopes, you see more and more of their descendants, a large part of the lowland population. These people speak English, making this coast an easy place to travel for those with limited Spanish.

Coffee has now been replaced by sugar cane and bananas, with some groves of cacao, the source of chocolate. At Siquirres, the first major town on the coastal plain, an electric engine replaces the diesel one and you notice the railroad ties are concrete instead of wood. As the train leaves the mountains, you follow the shores of the rushing, muddy Reventazón, occasionally crossing it or clear tributaries on bridges.

Some villages are built up on poles to keep from flooding. In one of the last villages, boardwalks run between houses and the only dry ground seems to be occupied by the cemetery. You pass the national oil refinery at Moin and railroad tracks joining from banana plantations to the north. For a few miles you follow the shore between palms and see breakers in the Caribbean on your left.

INCOFER

SAN JOSE — LIMON

N⁰ 696675

Hasta la estación última impresa abajo y en la fecha estampada. Debe ser presentado al Conductor del Tren cuando él lo requiera y no tendrá valor alguno si indicare haber sido alterado o mutilado.

Station	(inverted)
SAN JOSE	SAN JOSE
CARTAGO	CARTAGO
Paraíso	Paraíso
El Yas	El Yas
Santiago	Santiago
Las Mesas	Las Mesas
Juan Viñas	Juan Viñas
La Gloria	La Gloria
Chiz	Chiz
Murcia	Murcia
Las Pavas	Las Pavas
Florencia	Florencia
Turrialba	Turrialba
Río Jesús Ma.	Río Jesús Ma.
Torito	Torito
Peralta	Peralta
Tunel Camp.	Tunel Camp.
Casorla	Casorla
Bonilla	Bonilla
Pascua	Pascua
San Antonio	San Antonio
El Rubí	El Rubí
Las Lomas	Las Lomas
Florida	Florida
La Junta	La Junta
Siquirres	Siquirres
Pacuarito	Pacuarito
Monte Verde	Monte Verde
Cimarrones	Cimarrones
Río Hondo	Río Hondo
Madre de Dios	Madre de Dios
Waldeck	Waldeck
Bataán	Bataán
Margarita	Margarita
Matina	Matina
Estrada	Estrada
Zent	Zent
Boston	Boston
Saborío	Saborío
San Edmundo	San Edmundo
15 ½ Millas	15 ½ Millas
Toro	Toro
14 Millas	14 Millas
Bocas	Bocas
Búffalo	Búffalo
10 ½ Millas	10 ½ Millas
9 Millas	9 Millas
Liverpool	Liverpool
Cocal	Cocal
Esp. Castro	Esp. Castro
Sandoval	Sandoval
Miramar	Miramar
Refinadora	Refinadora
Moín	Moín
Emp. Moín	Emp. Moín
LIMON	LIMON

Train ticket from San Jose to Puerto Limon.

24

Finally the train pulls into Limón and you follow the crowd a few short blocks to the center of town where most hotels and the bus stops are.

Electric Train to West Coast

As thousands of cruise ship passengers have found, the electric narrow-gauge train from San Jose to Puntarenas is a delightful, scenic ride through farming country, along the gorge of the Barranca River, with stops at tiny villages not reached by highway or bus. While newer and not as historic as the Atlantic Railway, the Pacific Railway offers a beautiful half-day ride that is not as exhausting as the trip all the way to Limón and is much more scenic than the bus from San Jose to Puntarenas.

At its many stops villagers get on to go or come from market in Orotina, the only large town you pass. Going west, if you are on the left side of the train, you look down into the Barranca gorge as the train skirts steep ridges, turns tightly around canyons, sways through tunnels, and stops at a small station with a few houses or a ranch every few minutes. After Orotina the valley widens and you are soon down in the lowlands following the river and then the shore with stops at Mata Limón, Caldera, Chacarita, and several other villages on the way into Puntarenas.

The train leaves from the Ferrocarril Pacifica station on Ave. 20 at Calle 2 at 6 a.m. and 1 p.m. daily (check with ICT or the station about Sundays). Note that during Christmas shopping season it leaves at about 3 p.m. on the afternoon run and makes the last part of the trip in the dark. Fare is about $1.25, a real bargain for all that entertainment.

Jungle crowds both sides of the canales as we watch for sloths and monkeys.

"Los Canales"-Inland Waterway

From Moin, a few miles north of Puerto Limón, a jungle waterway extends over 65 miles up the northeast coast to Barra Colorado. Eight rivers form lagoons behind jungle-covered sandbars as they reach the ocean. By digging canals to connect them, the Costa Ricans have built a continuous water highway where there are no land roads. Fishing boats, skiffs, dugout canoes, coconut barges, a government boat and tour boats ply the scenic highway. Traffic varies seasonally according to water depth (less in February and March), fishing and crop seasons.

The ride is spectacular! You glide along a passage sometimes less than 100 feet wide between banks lined with palms and jungle. Water hyacinths cover water near the shores. Turtles sun themselves on logs and an occasional cayman splashes into the water just as you get your camera focussed. You pass a family of howler monkeys in a treetop and later a trio of brown spider monkeys swinging effortlessly from one limb to another. A dozen white egrets take off from a tree ahead. A huge blue-green kingfisher swoops beside the boat. The boat driver points at a treetop and you peer but don't see anything move. Nothing does—it's a sloth hanging spread-eagled by the front and back feet on the same side. At least there's no rush to get the picture. The tree's leaves move in the breeze, but the sloth doesn't.

Occasionally you pass a small farm or a thatched hut with a pig standing on the canal bank and a housewife washing clothes in the water. Standard yellow highway signs note the kilometers to villages at river intersections. At Parismina, Tortuguero, and Barra Colorado, there are fishing lodges where tarpon and snook fishermen fly in from San Jose for a few days to a week. Tortuguero is a village described in the Eastern region later in this book. If you're not on a tour going farther, you may want to stop over here. Just north of the village is the river mouth where waves break in the Caribbean. You turn left up another river channel and pass a hill on the right, the only one for miles. This is Tortuguero National Park, refuge for the green turtle, the manatee, and many other species. For more details, see the section on that park. Soon you leave the river and follow a palm-lined canal straight for miles with poetic reflections in the dark bog water. Against the afternoon sky a silhouette crosses ahead—it looks like a bird attached to a canoe—a toucan! The first time you see one outside a cage is a real thrill. Great blue herons and small night herons wade near shore until you approach before flying off.

A coco boat carries freight and passengers between Moin and villages along the canales.

27

This ride ends at the village of Barra Colorado, the mouth of the Rio Colorado. I hope border conditions will improve so you can continue on a tour boat or perhaps a local boat (though there is lots less traffic in that direction at any time) up the Rio San Juan, which forms the Costa Rican border, up the beautiful clear Sarapiqui to the village of Puerto Viejo and thence by rough road back to San Jose.

Presently your choices for the ride I've described are by tour boat, government launch ("La Samay"), or by making your own arrangements with freight boats. My first trip up this waterway was in a fast, narrow, and very unstable fish-hauling boat that makes the round trip from Barra to Moin and back in a day. Night came very black with rain showers as the driver peered through a slit in the plastic before him and steered around logs I couldn't see, occasionally switching on a dim flashlight to shine at boats we met. No navigation lights on shore here— any flashing light was a firefly! Cheapest and slowest are the "cocoboats" which haul coconuts to Moin and people with their shopping back. Built like powered barges, they make the African Queen look quite seaworthy. The government boat runs several days a week (starting very early in the morning from Moin) when water depth permits. It has a schedule which you may be able to get from the ICT office under the Cultural Plaza in San Jose. If you're using any of the other local boats, you need to have flexible enough time to allow an extra day or two in case there aren't any boats leaving north or south the day you want to go. Charter flights can be arranged from the airport in San Jose and the fishing lodges at Tortuguero and Barra Colorado use them.

Tourists and locals ride passenger boat up the canal.

28

Tour guide, Anita, from Rio Colorado Lodge, prepares lunch on boat.

Tour boats are the most predictable way to go if your trip is scheduled. They also stop for wildlife photos. The guides are looking for animals and know where they are most likely. Rio Colorado Lodge at Barra Colorado runs several trips weekly from San Jose on their modern tour boat, with a short stop at Tortuguero, using a mini-bus between San Jose and Moin and charter flights between Barra and San Jose. You may do this loop in either direction, depending on their schedule. The tour takes 2 days, but you can stay extra days at the lodge or ride the train to Limón, stay overnight, and join a tour there if you've booked it before leaving San Jose. Costa Rica Expeditons runs tours on the canales as far as Tortuguero to Tortuga Lodge, allowing time for canoeing up back channels of the river. Isla de Pesca, a fishing lodge at Barra Colorado, now has a tour boat running regularly to their lodge. The *Mwamba* travels the canales and does so quietly enough to allow seeing wildlife. I rode one time on *Gran Delta* the government boat, and speed plus noise made wildlife photography impossible though it was a cheap way to reach Tortuguero for several days of more leisurely viewing.

Note that some of the fishing lodges are only open for snook in the fall and tarpon in winter and early spring.

Rio Colorado Lodge and Barra Colorado village.

Fishing

Costa Rica has some of the world's finest sport fishing on both coasts and in streams and lakes. Depending on season and location, you can choose among tarpon, snook, marlin, sailfish, yellowfin tuna, roosterfish, wahoo, crevalle, snapper, or often hook several species in a day. In fresh water, rainbow trout have been planted, and bobo and guapote are native. The fishing lodges and sportfishing clubs hold tournaments (ICT has the dates).

Facilities are increasing for fishermen, with new lodges, more charter boats, and a large corps of knowledgeable guides on both coasts. For scuba fishermen, equipment and air refills are now available at major resorts on the west coast as well as in San Jose. You will need a fishing license which your lodge can get for you (they need your name, marital status, address, and passport number) or which you can get from the Dept. of Agriculture (Ministerio de Agricultura y Ganaderia, C. 1, Av. 1, San Jose, Costa Rica. Phone 23-08-29).

You should bring a wide-brimmed hat, long-sleeved shirts, long pants, and a good sunscreen. On the Caribbean coast, bring light rain wear all year. You are encouraged to bring your own gear, but lodges can arrange rentals. Generally for saltwater fishing, you need 20 lb. test line or stronger. ICT has a brochure on fishing that lists recommended lures. Your lodge can be more specific. The fishing columnist for the *Tico Times* sometimes publishes recommendations. The Caribbean coast is best known for tarpon and snook, with much of the fishing done from skiffs in river channels. Tarpon average 75 lbs., though larger ones are common. Fishermen rave about hooking more than a dozen a day even in November which is considered off-season. The main tarpon season is January through mid-May, though they are caught all year. However, even Archie Fields, owner of Rio Colorado Lodge, does not recommend the rains of December as enjoyable fishing weather.

Snook, a fine gamefish and good food, is caught on both coasts, near river mouths and from beaches. Peak season for large ones is from August to mid-October, but they are caught all year. Most fishing lodges are open only for the seasons listed above (see their descriptions in the Eastern region later in this book), except for the Rio Colorado Lodge. At Tortuguero, Sabina's Cabinas and other rooms are open all year and you could make your own fishing arrangements with a guide and skiff. The Tortuga Lodge is open all year with boats and fishing guides as well as nature touring in quiet back channels.

On the Pacific coast, sailfish and marlin are the most sought fish. Tamarindo and Coco Beaches both have boats and guides available, and most hotels anywhere along the coast can arrange deep-sea fishing. Sailfish average 100 lbs. but are often larger. Marlin can be huge, and are found from Golfito north. Peak seasons listed by Jerry Ruhlow in the *Tico Times* are as follows: Sailfish—July through September; roosterfish—year round but most caught in May and June; dorado (dolphinfish)—same as sailfish; wahoo—June through September; yellowfin tuna—July and August, but caught all year.

Freshwater fish seasons vary. Lake Arenal is especially popular for guapote (there is at least 1 tournament a year) and the season is open January 1 through September 30. Several areas feature trout fishing with fish originally planted, including the Chacon farm at San Gerardo, in the mountains below the Inter-American Highway.

The avid fisherman can find fish all year in Costa Rica and can find peak season for at least 1 species almost any time.

Travel agents in the United States and elsewhere book package tours to the fishing lodges and you will find the addresses of the lodges themselves in the Eastern, Northwestern, and Western sections later in this book.

Hunting

The days of unlimited sport hunting for jaguars and other exotic species are over in Costa Rica and most other places. As tropical forests everywhere are converted to crop or rangeland, the remaining habitat will not allow a surplus for hunting. Most species formerly hunted in Latin America are now threatened or endangered.

In Costa Rica there is legal hunting by permit for doves and ducks on the winter range—some of the same birds you see on spring and fall migrations in North America. The dryland rice fields of Guanacaste are   hunted,   from November through March. Hunters sometimes get 140 doves in a day, usually given to the nearby villagers for food. Hunters stay in or near Nicoya. For package tours or information, write Archie Fields, owner of the **Rio Colorado Lodge,** who holds permits for the area. His address and phone are listed in the information sources section.

Brasilito children play their favorite game.

River rafting is growing rapidly in Costa Rica, drawing people from many countries to rivers like the Reventazon, Pacuare, Chirripo, General, and Corobici.

Sports

Costa Ricans are avid sportsmen and have built many facilities throughout the country. Some are basic. A few are lavish. There are local and international tournaments in several sports, so you can be a spectator or participant according to your interests. Soccer (futbol)—almost every village with a bit of flat ground has a soccer field, often in front of the church. After work and on weekends, there's almost always play. Major games and tournaments are played at Sabana Park at the west end of San Jose. Newspaper sport sections always carry the latest soccer results.

Basketball—Is also popular, with major games played at the national gymnasium in Sabana Park. There are baskets for practice in the park and in most villages.

Swimming—Besides the beaches and rivers, most major hotels and apartotels have pools. Sabana Park has an Olympic-size pool, as does the Cariari Country Club. The pools fed by Oja de Agua spring south of Juan Santamaria Airport, are colder but unchlorinated due to the large supply of fresh water. There are major swim meets and a well-organized junior racing program at Sabana Park and the Cariari Country Club.

Surfing—A Banzai Pipeline hasn't been discovered yet in Costa Rica, but several beaches have **very** consistent waves that make good riding. Jacó Beach and Playa Herradura just north of it have hosted recent tournaments. As the sport takes hold here, you'll see much more. Windsurfing or board sailing is also growing. Playa Hermosa on the northwest coast features a full range of watersports and equipment rented by **Aqua Sport**, 67-00-50. If you call **Diving Safaris**, 24-00-33, in San Jose, they could give you good tips for other areas. For cool water and wind, almost guaranteed to be at least 25 knots every afternoon, we recommend Lake Arenal. You'd probably want some cold protection, but the lake is 14 miles long and always windy!

Scuba and snorkeling—Costa Rica has good snorkeling on both coasts. Cahuita, south of Puerto Limón, has the only coral reef on the Caribbean coast, complete with sunken Spanish ship. A few miles south, at Puerto Viejo, snorkeling is good in the bay in front of town. There are presently no air refills available on the coast for scuba. On the west coast at Playa Hermosa, **Aqua Sports** rents equipment, including sailboards, and has boats and guides. They are only a few miles from the Islas Murciélagos, one of the best diving areas in Costa Rica, accessible only by boat. **Diving Safaris** in San Jose runs trips to both coasts and has equipment.

I have found snorkeling good on rocky points near many beaches such as Playa Coco, but to get really clear water with 80 ft. or more visibility, you need to go offshore, away from farming and erosion. Off the northwest coast, the Islas Murciélagos, and off the Osa Peninsula in the southwest, Caño Island are such places. **Marenco** and **Phantom Island Lodge** provide tours to the island, and the latter has scuba gear and refills. The best diving in Costa Rica is at Cocos Island, over 300 miles west of the mainland. It is a national park, with no facilities onshore. The yacht, *Victoria*, sailing from Puntarenas is the only tourist access unless you have your own long range boat. Anywhere you go on the coast, it's fun to have a snorkel and see what you can find. In most places there are none on the coast, so you may want to bring a mask and snorkel.

Golf—Cariari Country Club, a few miles west of San Jose, has the only 18-hole golf course in Costa Rica. Designed by a major golf course architect, it's the site of international tour-

Don Humberto Ruiz in Escazu breeds and trains Andalusian horses in dressage. This classic Spanish breed was the foundation of the Lippizan and Paso Fino horses.

naments featuring many PGA pros. There are also 4 9-hole courses: at the Costa Rican Country Club in Escazú, surrounding the Golfito Airport, at Los Reyes Country Club near Alajuela, and at El Castillo Country Club above Heredia. Most have equipment available. The course at Golfito is not being well-maintained since the banana company left and may not be playable. At presstime a new course was being built at Tango Mar on the south coast of the Nicoya peninsula near Play Tambor.

Tennis—Several of the deluxe hotels have courts as do Sabana Park, the nearby Costa Rica Tennis Club, the Cariari Country Club (where the World Friendship Tournament is played in March and April), the Costa Rica Country Club, and the Los Reyes Country Club. The Costa Rica Tennis Club and Sabana Park courts are close to San José.

Horseback riding—Costa Rica raises very fine jumpers and parade horses, notably Andalusian and Paso Fino horses with the soft gait prized by the Spaniards. On early mornings in the suburbs of Santa Ana and Escazú, you may see them in the streets. During Christmas week, there is the Horse Parade in downtown San José with over 1000 of the country's finest. Near San José, you can take instruction and ride at Hipico La Carana, about 15 miles west of the city, and at the Cariari Country Club. At Cariari, jumping, equitation, and dressage are featured with expert instruction and 4 to 7 day clinics. Horseshows are frequent. Elsewhere you can rent country horses, and many hotels will arrange it for you. Note that on the coasts where it is often hot, riding early or late may be more fun than at midday.

Rodeos and Bullfights—Guanacaste is the cattle country of Costa Rica, with the festivals and sports that go with it. Rodeos and bullfights are frequent during the dry season from November to April, in Santa Cruz, Nicoya, and Liberia. In Costa Rican bullfights, the bull is not killed, and the whole show is for fun! During Christmas holidays, there are rodeos and bullfights in San José. Rodeos are also held at the Cariari Country Club.

Bicycling—Bicycle touring and racing is a major sport in Costa Rica. The big event of the year is the "Vuelta a Costa Rica" in December, lasting 12 days and criscrossing the mountain backbone of the country several times, from sea level to over 11,000 feet. It attracts cyclists from many countries, including the United States. The Recreational Cycling Association plans family outings which many join on Sundays.

A friend who has cycled long distances here says that drivers are more considerate of cyclists than he expected and give room when passing. He warns that one needs to be prepared for heat and great temperature changes with altitude. He carries liquids and a gas mask for long grades also used by diesel trucks and buses. Despite heat and fumes at times, he recommends cycling in Costa Rica.

Other Sports—Wrestling, in the national gymnasium at Sabana Park, car and motorcycle racing at La Guacima near Alajuela, volleyball everywhere, baseball and Little League programs, and jogging for everyone on the paths at Sabana Park are a few of the other sports you can watch and participate in.

Melico Salazar Theater, facing Parque Central in San Jose, was recently restored. Many plays and musical events are performed here.

Theater and Museums

These are almost all in San Jose or its suburbs, though historical and archeological sites are scattered throughout the country.

The National Theater is Costa Rica's symbol of the people's interest in the arts as well as the national architectural treasure.

A European opera company, led by singer Adelina Patti, came to Guatemala City in the late 1800's but didn't travel on to Costa Rica because there was no suitable place to perform. In response, the coffee growers agreed to pay a tax on coffee they exported to raise money for a theater. Construction started in 1890 and the building was finished in 1897.

Today it is one of the busiest buildings in the country, with performances or official functions 320 days a year. If your Spanish is good, enjoy one of the many plays presented by Costa Rican and touring foreign companies. With little or no Spanish, you can watch dance performances, opera, or the National Symphony. Check the schedule of upcoming events so you won't miss the ones you'd like during your stay. Tickets are amazingly inexpensive, many under $2.

The theater is patterned after European opera houses though on a smaller, more comfortable scale. The facade, overlooking a rose garden and a tree-shaded square, is Renaissance style, with figures representing Music, Fame, and Dance. Statues of Beethoven and Calderon de la Barca fill niches on either side of the entrance. The lobby inside has marble floors and columns. To your left is a refreshment area with coffee and great ice cream concoctions, its walls usually adorned with art exhibits. The grand staircase and foyer on the second floor feature Italian marble sculptures, paintings and a mural of Costa Rica's main exports. You can tour the building with or without a guide during the day, but shouldn't miss the experience of a performance. Av. 2, C.3., adjacent to the Cultural Plaza and Gran Hotel Costa Rica.

The National Theater adjoins the south side of the Cultural Plaza and faces the same square as the Gran Hotel Costa Rica. Other smaller theaters are around the San Jose area and the University of Costa Rica campus. Check the English language Tico Times, weekly on Fridays, for performances, locations and for art exhibits in the city which change often.

The National Museum of Costa Rica is in the old army barracks on Calle 17, Avenida 2/ctl (see the San Jose section for an explanation of San Jose street addresses). Phones, 22-12-29 and 21-02-95. Open Tuesday through Saturday, 8:30 to 5:00. Closed Mondays, Sundays and holidays, 9:00 to 5:00. Small admission fee. Students with identification free. The outside walls of this fortress still show bullet scars from the revolution of 1948, after which the army was abolished. The museum features an excellent exhibit of pre-Columbian artifacts, historical exhibits from the colonial period, and historical religious costumes and articles. All of Costa Rica's history and historical art are represented here in the massive stone buildings surrounding a garden.

A prehistoric basalt ball several feet in diameter lies in front of the bullet-scarred fortress that is now the National Museum.

The Jade Museum features prehistoric carvings of jade and stone, and some ceramic and gold articles, arranged according to their region and historical period. It's on the 11th floor of the INS (Institute for National Security) Building, Calle 9, Av. 7. Phone, 23-58-00. Open Tuesday through Sunday, 8:00 to 5:00. Admission free. Despite the hours listed above, I was told it was too late when I tried to enter once at 3 p.m. You should probably call ahead or check with the ICT office under the Cultural Plaza.

Note that most museum openings are early in Costa Rica. Closings sometimes are as well. Most museums are open on Sundays—sometimes admission free. Most, except for the Natural Science Museum, are closed Mondays.

The Gold Museum is near the ICT information center under the Cultural Plaza on Av. Central. At presstime it was closed until funds could be raised for more security facilities. This collection, one of the finest in the world, contains over 1600 pieces of all sizes and types. Its 24,000 troy ounces are the second largest collection in the Western Hemisphere. The artistic wealth as well as the gold make it well worth a visit. Many of the articles were obtained from private collections of burial and religious art.

The National Art Museum occupies the former airport terminal building in Sabana Park on Calle 42 at the west end of Paseo Colon, Phones, 23-60-87 and 22-86-04. Open Tuesdays through Sundays, 10:00 to 5:00. Closed Mondays. In this lovely Spanish-style building is a great collection of some of the most expressive art you'll ever see. Most is modern, but some sculptures are pre-Columbian. There are changing exhibits as well as the permanent collection.

The Natural Science Museum is in the Colegio La Salle, a school at the southwest of Sabana Park. Phone 32-64-27. Open Mondays through Fridays, 8:00 to 3:00. Small admission charge. All specimens and scenes were prepared locally, though they feature species from around the world as well as Costa Rica.

The Entomology Museum in Sabanilla Montes de Oca, an eastern suburb of San Jose, is the only insect museum in Central America. The butterflies alone would be worth a trip. Phone 25-55-55. Hours not known. Call the museum or ask the ICT.

A small farmer's home in the mountains south of the Central Valley, surrounded by flowering shrubs and trees.

COSTA RICA—THE NATION
Geography and Climate

With a land area of about 19,700 square miles, Costa Rica is the second smallest country in Central America, after El Salvador. Its rapidly growing population of about 2½ million is the second smallest as well, after Panama. It forms a land bridge with coasts on both the Atlantic and Pacific Oceans between Nicaragua and Panama.

The Atlantic Coast is a lowland, rather straight and with few good harbors, about 125 miles long. The Pacific Coast has 2 deep bays formed by the Nicoya and Osa Peninsulas, and is over 600 miles long. The ports of Puntarenas, with the new port at Caldera just to the south, and Golfito in the southwest corner of the country are in these bays. Many of the beaches we've mentioned line this coast.

Costa Rica has a mountainous backbone running the length of the country with just one very significant break, the Meseta

41

Central or Central Valley. The northern mountains are a chain of volcanoes extending south from Nicaragua, including the Cordilleras Guanacaste, Tilarán and Central. Within this chain are active and dormant volcanoes, thermal springs, and many cinder cones. It's a very active zone with eruptions, earthquakes and some moving lava flows. South of the Meseta Central is the Talamanca Range topped by Cerro Chirripó over 12,600 ft. high, continuing south into Panama.

The Meseta Central is by far the most important area of the country though it's only about 15 by 40 miles. This rolling area of rich volcanic soils has a spring climate all year thanks to its altitude of about 4,000 feet. Frost never happens and the main seasonal variation is rain. Temperatures vary widely according to altitude, with a few hundred feet making a real difference. There two-thirds of the people live and it's one of the most heavily populated areas in Latin America.

Some people have described Costa Rica as "the Meseta Central and everywhere else." The bustling capital of San Jose, with 275,000 people in 1983, and the nearby towns of Heredia, Alajuela, Cartago and Turrialba, plus a swarm of smaller villages, are indeed the center of government, industry, agriculture, and the most important, outlook, of Costa Rica.

South of the Meseta Central, bordering the western flank of the Talamanca Mountains, is the Valle de General, with its principal town of San Isidro de General. While it is much lower and warmer than the Meseta Central, it isn't as crowded, and many farmers have moved into the area recently since the Inter-American Highway and the new road down the west coast from Esparza have connected this area more closely to domestic and international trade. No roads cross the Talamancas and few lead far into them.

The Nicoya and Osa Peninsulas have central ranges of hills to 3,000 ft., with some of the Nicoya hills being quite steep. The western coastal plain is generally rolling rather than truly flat, and extends from the Panamanian border northward, widening to form the cattle and rice country of Guanacaste, to the Nicaraguan border. Similarly, the eastern plain widens from south to north, forming a wide northern and eastern lowland north of Puerto Limon. The lowlands have a limited population, mostly in agriculture, few large towns, but do have some larger fincas or plantations.

Costa Rica extends from 8 degrees to 11 degrees north of the Equator, so the sun is never far from overhead (it actually passes over during May and September). The length of daylight hours varies only slightly all year and the average daily temperature in a given location may vary only a few degrees throughout the year. In San Jose, the daily highs are in the 70's, Fahrenheit, almost all year. Alajuela, just a few hundred feet lower, averages a few degrees warmer, while Limón and Puntarenas at sea level are usually in the high 80's or 90's during "summer", December through March. March and April are the warmest months and can be hot, even in the capital. There is much greater variation, especially in the mountains, between day and night temperatures at the same place. You will usually want a sweater or jacket at night in San Jose, and I wore one on a rainy night in a leaky boat in the Tortuguero Canals at sea level.

Altitude rather than season really controls temperature here. Frosts do occur on Chirripó, and most of the country above 6500 ft. is in cloud forest, cool with fog or rain brought by the northeast trade winds. Mornings are ofter clear in the mountains, with clouds building in early afternoon.

Those of you who've joined the metric world will find the distances, altitudes and temperatures as given in Costa Rica easy. This U. S. resident has not yet learned to think metric and so will use miles, feet, and Fahrenheit, with apologies for any confusion.

Rainy and dry seasons and the amount of rainfall are controlled by the northeast trades, and the doldrums (a tropical zone of rising air which follows the sun north and south), and the mountain chain running through Costa Rica. The dry season in San Jose and the West is usually December into April (May in Guanacaste) while it runs from January to April on the Atlantic Coast. While the east coast is wetter, some areas on the west get extra rain because of being aligned with passes which allow the moist winds through. A station in the eastern mountains reported rain on 359 days in one year! However, on the drier northwest coast, there are few rainy days even in the wet season, and the rain then is generally in late afternoon or night.

Even rainy season shouldn't stop you if you allow for it. On October mornings in San Jose, I enjoyed the clear moist air, Poás Volcano with its steam plume against the blue sky, and flocks of chattering parrots passing overhead. All morning and much of the afternoon stayed dry, though clouds gathered. By late afternoon almost every day, the sky burst. Everone still out unfolded the umbrellas they always carried. I liked sitting on the roofed porch watching the rain gauge fill and overflow.

Golfito in the southwest actually has a climate much like the Caribbean coast, due to the mountains vs. the winds. One December evening there even an umbrella didn't help much in the 4 inches of rain that fell in 2 hours, but it was warm and the rain cooled the town after a hot sunny day.

Paddling a dugout canoe in the canal.

Costa Rican Holidays

January 1, New Year's Day
March 19, St. Joseph
Easter, 3 days (at least)
April 11, Battle of Rivas
May 1, Labor Day
June, Corpus Christi
June 29, St. Peter and St. Paul
July 25, Guanacaste Day, celebrating its annexation.
August 2, Virgin of Los Angeles
August 15, Mother's Day
September 15, Independence Day
October 12, Columbus Day
December 8, Conception of the Virgin
December 25, Christmas Day

While these are the official days, during Christmas holiday week between Christmas and New Year's, and during Easter Holy week, from Wednesday noon through Sunday, most of the country seems to be shut down. Not only are banks and offices closed, but buses don't run on some days, meaning that you need to plan ahead where you will be, with reservations, and how you will get around. If you want to see San Jose when the only moving traffic is religious processions, try Good Friday. Those who can take vacation then do so, and the more accessible beaches are jammed. Columbus Day is the time of annual festival in Limón, and the August 2 holiday of the Virgin of Los Angeles is Cartago's biggest festival. Some celebrants march from San Jose to Cartago!

In Santa Maria de Dota, this monument commemorates the heroes of the revolution of 1948.

45

Seasons & Activities Table

SEASONS & ACTIVITIES	D	J	F	M	A	M	J	J	A	S	O	N
Rainy season, San Jose					--	x	x	x	x	x	x	x
Dry season, San Jose	x	x	x	x	x--							
Rainy season, Guanacaste					--	x	x	x	x	x	x	x
Dry season, Guanacaste	x	x	x	x	x--							
Rainy season, Limón	x	x			x	x		x			x	x
Dry season, Limón			x	x			x		x	x		
Independence Day										15		
Carnivals	S.J					Punt.				Limón		
Horse Shows	S.J											
Rodeos, Guanacaste		18	x					25				
Bullfights		18	x					25				
Tarpon, East Coast		x	x	x	x	x	x	x	x	x	x	x
Snook, East Coast		x	x	x	x	x	x	x	x	x	x	x
Marlin, West Coast	x	x	x	x	x	x	x	x	x	x	x	x
Sailfish, West Coast	←------- NORTH -------→					←------- SOUTH -------→						
Tortuguero												
Green Turtles, egglaying								x	x	x		
Green Turtles, hatching								x	x	x		
Guanacaste												
Leatherback, egg laying	X	X	X	X								X
Leatherback, hatching	X	X	X	X								
Ridley egg laying	X										x	X
Ridley hatching	x											x
Dove hunting, Guanacaste	x	x	x	x								x
Duck hunting, Guanacaste	x	x	x	x								x

A replica of Columbus's ship built for a film about Columbus's voyage and landing near Puerto Limon in 1502.

History

This section will give only the briefest outline of Costa Rican history, to give some perspective to what you will see. For more information and an excellent discussion of social and political conditions, you could read *The Costa Ricans* by Richard, Karen and Mavis Biesanz, who have lived in Costa Rica for years.

Before the Spaniards came, Costa Rica had several dozen independent tribes who apparently didn't form the empires that the Mayas, Aztecs, and Incas did to the north and south of them. They did some farming and did have some permanent settlements which are still being studied. The sculptures and ceramic figues you can see in museums show that they had artists and had developed culture.

In 1502, Columbus landed at Cariari, now Puerto Limón, and stayed for several days. The Indians showed his men some gold and he felt there was hope for more.

However, the small tribes hadn't accumulated the wealth that drew the Spaniards to the bigger empires. Warfare between the tribes and with the Spaniards plus the diseases brought by the

47

white men to which the natives had no immunity nearly wiped out the native population.

The Spanish who came and settled found both coasts had a hot, humid climate and tropical diseases which many couldn't tolerate. The coasts were also raided by pirates of many countries, especially British, who sacked and burned whatever the settlers had. There were no easy routes to the interior, but eventually small farmers did settle up in the cool, healthful climate of the Meseta Central.

Unlike the other Spanish colonies, these settlers had no way to amass great wealth, no natives to enslave, and few to inter-marry. These farmers remained almost pure Spanish and didn't develop the social classes or the mestizo majority that charac-terized most of New Spain. They were almost forgotten by Spain since they had little to trade and no wealth to send back to Europe. Even the access routes to their settlements mostly led up from the west coast instead of the east.

Cartago was the main town, started in 1563, but San Jose wasn't established until 1737, Heredia in 1717. The population, mostly poor and still struggling, hadn't grown enough to settle the whole valley, though they had brought some fine cattle and horses from Spain and continued to grow livestock and food crops.

In the late 1700s, coffee was introduced, and with the rich volcanic soils and near perfect climate, it was a winner! Land was given to those who would plant it for an export crop. Even though the coffee had to be carried by oxcart west to Puntarenas and thence around Cape Horn or across Panama, Costa Rica finally began to grow in population and wealth.

In 1821, the Spanish colonies declared independence from Spain. Various attempts were made to unify the former colonies in the Central American Federation which Costa Rica joined in 1824 and from which she withdrew in 1838. The lack of rapid communication, as well as differing interests, made a unified regional government very difficult, though economic and po-litical treaties based on regional interest had been signed.

Coffee growth and trade led some families to become richer and more powerful than others, and Costa Rica was no longer a classless society. It was still a group of small towns and farms with little feeling of nationality. The town councils met separately and rivalries grew until San Jose won a battle with Cartago and the capital was moved to San Jose in 1823.

Democracy developed with some setbacks according to the personalities of those who were elected chief of state, and then president after 1847. Some of the most autocratic leaders are remembered for starting schools and getting roads and railroads built. Juan Rafael Mora, president 1849-59, recruited an army of volunteers which marched from San Jose to Santa Rosa (now a national park) to surround and drive out pro-slavery American William Walker and his band of filibusters who were trying to establish a slavery empire in Central America. Walker and his band were driven back into Nicaragua and again defeated at the Battle of Rivas.

National hero, Juan Santamaria, was a youth from Alajuela who volunteered to torch the building Walker and his men occupied, knowing it was a suicide mission. Walker was later captured in Honduras, held by the British, and turned over to Honduran authorities who executed him. President Mora's proclamation of the rights of the Costa Rican people to be free of foreign despots is respected by Costa Ricans as U.S. citizens respect the Declaration of Independence.

In 1889, for the first time, Costa Rica's election was not controlled by the party in power (nearly a hundred years later, many other nations still haven't reached this point). Later administrations have passed laws establishing national health insurance, labor rights, and property rights.

The last internal military strife was in 1948 when the party in power tried to use the army to remain so after losing an election. A volunteer group led by Jose Figueres took Cartago, and after widespread violence and bloodshed, a cease-fire was arranged. Costa Ricans were determined this should never happen again. Among the changes Figueres and his followers enacted were limitations on the length of presidential terms and elimination of the army. A well-armed and trained national guard serves as the country's police force. Its control is turned

Juan Santamaria, a boy from Alajuela, gave his life to burn the building William Walker held in the Battle of Rivas, becoming Costa Rica's national hero.

over to the election tribunal before national elections to remove it from politics and guarantee free elections.

Costa Rica celebrates the fortieth anniversary of the constitution Nov. 7, 1988, justifiably proud of 40 years of free elections, democracy, and survival without an army in Latin America! President Oscar Arias proposed a peace plan for Central America which was adopted, with modifications by all the Central American governments in August 1987. Its success will only be known later, but for his effort he was awarded the Nobel Peace Prize in 1987. Costa Rica's contribution to peace and democracy is very big for so small a nation.

In recent years, the population, size of bureaucracy, and foreign debt have grown rapidly. With almost all exports in the form of raw agricultural products, Costa Rica is at the mercy of the world prices for them and for the oil it needs. The International Monetary Fund places stringent conditions on economic policy in an effort to control the foreign debt. Costa Rica is spending most of its income from foreign trade to pay the interest on that debt, a heavy burden on a country with many other needs. The traveler who checks prices in stores will quickly discover the difference between products from Central America and those imported.

Meanwhile, the turmoil in the Central American countries to the north and the resulting refugee flow into Costa Rica have added tension in the country. These people are keenly aware that they have advantages in education, personal freedom, and the possibility for personal progress that few in Latin America have. Many other countries now provide research funds, economic aid, and increased trade.

Social Conditions

"Tell them Costa Rica is different," many people said, from truck drivers to government department heads. They're right. Where else can you see this from 20,000 feet? Fly over El Salvador and you'll see big fields with a cluster of small houses and one big house. Fly over Costa Rica and you'll see many small fields and villages with houses that look similar from that distance, especially in the Meseta Central. Plantations owned by the banana companies and some of the cattle fincas in Guanacaste are an exception, but not as prevalent as in the other countries.

A walk through San Jose will show you that there are rich and poor here, but most people are middle class. Costa Rica has the largest proportion of middle class in Latin America. That, coupled with its high literacy rate (elementary and secondary education are free and elementary attendance is required) are the foundation of its democracy. Ride a public bus at evening rush hour and you'll see everyone reading newspapers.

Ticos, as the Costa Ricans call themselves, are very clean and very well-dressed. Their families, usually large, are all-important in their lives. For many, the extended family is the source of all their social life. Children are loved extravagantly and with

51

endless patience. You rarely see a crying child. They grow up to be cheerful, considerate people who will do anything to help you—as long you're polite. They aren't subservient. Cheerful self-respect you'll see everywhere, among the Spanish in the Meseta Central, the Indians and mestizos of Guanacaste, and the blacks of the Caribbean coast.

This Monteverde girl shows the beauty Costa Rican women are famous for.

Costa Rica is not immune to the human problems of the 20th century or of the developing nations. It is a nation of hard-working people who from earliest colonial times have struggled to make as good a life as possible for themselves and their families. Compared with the TV generation in other places, their resourcefulness in having fun on a minimum of money is impressive. With their families at home or on outings, they find fun or make it.

Population growth and the conversion of field agriculture to cattle range and bananas to palm nuts which take less labor have forced many into cities and towns looking for work. Everywhere there is a serious shortage of low-cost housing, though the government has built thousands of units near San Jose. In the outlying areas, and particularly among the people of the

Caribbean coast, there is a distrust of what the government and population majority in the Meseta Central may do that affects their life and land. Many women, especially the younger ones, feel caught between the traditional Spanish stereotype of the submissive role and the opportunites that are (or they feel should be) open to them. More women are studying for the professions, especially law. The San Jose area is more liberal than the conservative countryside in the choices open to women. You will find many in offices, occasionally even as "la directora."

As I noted earlier, Costa Rica is dedicated to solving these problems and has done much to make its citizens' lives better. Some solutions may wait until the growth of population and the bureaucracy is slowed.

Agriculture

Early agriculture in the tropics was the slash and burn type, with small areas of forest cut and planted for a few years before the soil was depleted and the farmer cleared another plot. Heavy tropical rains and the rapid breakdown of compost at these temperatures limit fertility unless fertilizers are added or crops rotated, or a volcano periodically adds mineral-rich ash to the upper layer. In prehistoric times, people moved on, allowing the soil and vegetation to restore themselves. Very steep hillsides were hard to work and didn't produce well, so they were farmed only if easier ground wasn't available.

Modern farms stay in the same place and most crops leave bare ground exposed to the heavy tropical rains. If it slopes, tons of soil are lost every year, even from steep pastures. Pressed by population and a growing international debt, Costa Rica has cut half her forests in the past 40 years. Before the year 2000 she will have used all forests not in parks and reserves. Where the soil is gone, forest cannot regrow. The government and even the Peace Corps are doing reforestation, but usually in quick-growing species like pine and eucalyptus which make firewood but do not make food for wildlife or restore the hundreds of species that grow in a tropical rainforest. Lately a few of the tropical hardwoods, including pochote, have been planted. The Costa Rican govern-ment recognizes the problem and is working on it. If you are concerned, you'll find suggestions in our "So You Want to Help" section.

53

Coffee blooms in March and April.

Coffee and bananas were the first two major exports of Costa Rica. Coffee still makes up 20% of the country's agricultural production though it's concentrated in a small proportion of the land and subject to wild price fluctuations on the world market. Throughout the Meseta Central, you'll see the glossy green bushes, often shaded by scattered trees. In season, the white blossoms or red berries add to the beauty.

Picking coffee in November is family work.

54

Bananas were first grown on the east coast along the railroad during construction, partly to help pay for completion of the project. That was the start of the United Fruit Company. Later, the Panama disease damaged many plantations and new planting was done on the southwest coast. Some western plantations are now being converted to oil palm—for oil used in margarine and soap. You may want to try varieties of bananas you can find in markets here which have much more flavor than the bombproof ones bred for shipping overseas. They make good snacks to take on buses and trains.

In the past 20 years, beef has become the fifth largest export, grown mostly in the west. Cattle are Brahma purebred or cross, bred to take heat and insects. Dairy cattle are raised mostly in the highlands usually above the Meseta Central or at Monteverde. Almost all the beef is grass-fed and relatively lean, exported mostly for fast-food hamburgers and TV dinners. Costa Rica desperately needs foreign exchange, but she is paying a high price for it. Cutting and burning forest from hills so steep a friend noticed "cows falling out of their pastures" on the road to Monteverde, cattle growers are responsible for much of the deforestation. Some cattle fincas in Guanacaste use introduced African grasses and modern methods to increase production on flatter ground.

Sugar cane has long been a major crop for home use and export. You'll see it along the road and railroad in the eastern Meseta Central. There it grows between coffee fields until it becomes the major crop as you drop down past Turrialba and into banana country. Other export crops are pineapples, copra and dried coconuts, cacao, cotton. Rice is a major crop in the west, all of it used in the country as it's a staple in the local diet. Also grown for local consumption are beans, corn, honey, vegetables, mangoes, papayas and many other tropical fruits, pork, chickens, and potatos, mostly on the slopes of Irazú.

House plants and cut flowers, grown under acres of plastic screening for shade and rain protection, are a new export crop in the Meseta Central. The plants in your office or home may have been grown in Costa Rica. It's fun to visit these places and see the plants you keep in little pots at home growing by the acre! Cut flowers, particularly carnations and chrysanthemums, grow under screening even on high ridges along the Inter-American Highway. Such crops require little land but much labor in a frost-free climate, ideal for Costa Rica.

Lately, there have been several developments promoting new export crops—oranges for juice concentrate, jojoba for oil, and macadamia nuts, to name several, If you stay in deluxe San Jose hotels, you'll be offered information about investments in these.

Cowboys drive cattle to pasture in Guanacaste past formerly forested hills now burned off for grass.

Industry

Costa Rica is one of the world's largest per capita producers of hydroelectric power with big installations at Lakes Arenal and Cachí. It exports electric power to several other Central American countries. Though there has been some oil exploration and talk of a trans-Costa Rican pipeline to transport Alaskan and Venezuelan oil, presently there is no oil produced in the country, which has made balancing the economy difficult.

Costa Rica offers tax incentives to labor-intensive industries producing items for export. Several plants import textiles, hire Costa Ricans to assemble them, and export finished products such as underwear. My uniform shirts on the Alaska ferry say "assembled in Costa Rica". One successful operator imports used typewriters from North America, reconditions them in a modern plant and exports them wholesale all over Latin America. There's plenty of room for imagination here! There are many products that Costa Rica would rather produce internally than pay foreign exchange for, but with a well-scattered population only as big as a large city, there isn't the market to make it pay.

The major non-agricultural industry (aside from government) is tourism. While numbers have dropped recently due to political problems to the north, Costa Rica has attractions and enough tourist facilities including hotels, restaurants and tour operators to handle many more. Costa Rica has so much to offer the tourist, and does it so well, that it is rapidly being discovered by thousands who ride jets instead of tossing Spanish galleons.

PLANNING YOUR TRIP

Do you hope to see as much as possible in the time you have for this trip, or would you rather "sit and watch the coconuts fall," as a relaxed friend in sleepy Puerto Viejo put it?

On my first trip to Costa Rica, I had not had a vacation in 8 years and really needed to get away from lists of things I had to do. I chose Costa Rica because it was an interesting place I hadn't been, with lots of birds and wildlife where no one shot at you. If the tropical heat proved too much after years of living in Alaska, I could go up to the cloud forests and look for quetzals. Planning for everything from snorkeling to high altitudes of course made packing harder.

San Jose, nearly in the center of the country, is a well-located base for touring. With 23 days to spend, I flew into San Jose and spent several days there learning my way around and getting bus, train, and boat schedules. Almost any hotel in San Jose will store extra baggage while you travel if they know you're coming back to stay there. Leaving dressy and warmer clothes there, I traveled a lop-sided figure 8 with a loop on each coast, and returned to San Jose for a few days in the middle and at the end of of my trip. From San Jose, I rode public buses up Irazú and Posá, toured Cartago and Alajuela, and went to the bird zoo. In San Jose, I toured museums, the national zoo, and attended performances of the National Symphony and a Venezuelan dance troupe in the National Theater.

I rode the train to Puerto Limón, spent a night there, and rode the bus to the village of Cahuita. It was so peaceful that I spent 4 days, staying in a primitive, but clean cabina, snorkeling and birdwatching in the national park. Back by bus in Limón for another night because there wasn't any boat that day. Then up the canales for 2 days at Barra Colorado before riding boat and bus back to San Jose.

The electric train west to Puntarenas didn't go when I wanted to, so I rode the bus and spent 2 night there. I enjoyed the Calypso tour in the Gulf of Nicoya and caught the early morning ferry the next day to the Nicoya Peninsula. There are more direct routes to Liberia and Santa Rosa National Park, but I wanted to see the country. The bus dropped me at the park entrance and I hiked into the campground and spent 3 days hiking, swimming, and wildlife watching before returning by bus to San Jose.

I've never seen so much or learned so much in 23 days! However, my stops for several days helped keep the trip from being a race. With all that travel and camping out just 2 nights, I spent an average of $17 a day for everything but souvenirs. You can spend a great deal more, or somewhat less if you stay more in one place. What are your interests? What kind of trip do you want?

Exchange

Please note: you need the current exchange rate compared to your own currency to plan and budget your trip. That rate was 75 Costa Rican colones per U.S. dollar during most of the hotel research for this book. Since most tourist hotels quote their rates in dollars, the price doesn't go down when currency is devalued slightly. For the past several years, the Costa Rican government has devalued the currency in small steps at about 12% a year, nearly matching inflation. You can learn the current rate from the nearest Costa Rican consulate or embassy, or by calling the Costa Rican Tourist Board office in Miami, (800)327-7033 from the U.S. , (305)358-2150 from Florida and elsewhere. Address: 1101 Brickell Ave., Suite 801, B.I.V. Tower, Miami, FL 33131.

As we go to press, the exchange has been raised to 85 colones per dollar. You can legally exchange money only at banks or hotels where you are staying. Penalties for exchanging money otherwise are severe and not worth the risk. The banks will charge a commission to exchange travelers' checks but not cash. You may want to carry some cash, carefully, in U.S. dollars, especially for airport taxes and baggage chargeswhen you may have used up your colones before leaving, or for arrivals on holidays or after bank closing hours. If you will arive during the latter part of Easter Week or between Christmas and New Years when the whole banking system is closed, you could try to exchange some money at your airport of departure for Costa Rica.

Travelers' checks and currency in U.S. dollars can be exchanged in any good-sized town, while other currencies may have to be exchanged at a particular bank, usually in San Jose. Banco Nacional in San Jose will change German marks for colones on working days, but on holidays you might not find any place open to exchange them. You will only be able to cash U.S. $50 back from colones into dollars when you leave, so you may want to have some travelers' checks in small denominations so you come out fairly even. If you will be staying in villages, you should carry some colones in small bills, as even a 100 colon note (about $1.11) can be hard to break. Major U.S. credit cards can be used for car rentals, excess baggage charges, and moderate to expensive hotels. They are often the simplest way to get funds from home if you run short.

On Costa Rican holidays the bank office at the airport is closed and **no one** else there will change colones back to dollars as you leave. You can buy gifts at the airport shops and pay your departure fee, about $6, in colones.

Safety

What are you to think when the American press refers to the political and military problems of Guatemala, El Salvador and Nicaragua as "Central America"? At least it's better than the former practice of calling everything between Mexico and Peru "banana republics." Even with the problems to the north, Costa Rica remains peaceful with great determination. Its democracy and neutrality together with lack of an army are its greatest sources of national pride. While residents are concerned about problems to the north, at presstime, no one I met felt that there was any chance of Costa Rica getting involved. One California paper headlined its article "What's a Nice Little Country Like Costa Rica Doing in a Place Like This?"—and then told what a delightful, relaxing place it is. During a Costa Rican vacation you probably won't see any evidence of the problems in other Central American countries.

There is far less violence in the entire country in a month than there is in any major U. S. city in a night. You are personally as least as safe here as you would be anywhere on earth, including at home.

Theft has always been here and has increased with the economic crisis and the admission of thousands of refugees who have not been able to find work. The bars across ground floor windows of most houses and other buildings will probably startle you on your first drive into San Jose from the airport. The vast majority of the people you see are the most honest people in the world, but here, as elsewhere, there are some of the others—and they are very quick and expert. I always take the precautions listed below.

1. When traveling, always look as neat and clean as humanly possible—but don't look affluent. Lots of jewelry and matched sets of leather luggage may make you feel more important when you arrive at a hotel, but unless you have Princess Diana's security forces, they aren't worth it. At best, you are a mark for every cab driver and merchant who can raise his price. At worst, you are an easy target for major theft. In particular, gold

neck chains with pendants and pierced earrings of any value are likely to be taken off you in the street (with possible damage to neck or ears). I never wear an expensive-looking watch, and keep cameras out of sight unless using them.

2. Try to avoid taking more luggage than you can carry at one time. Besides making travel easier, this saves leaving anything behind when moving through airline and bus terminals. Backpacks are handy, but avoiding a hippy look can save a lot of trouble with customs and unpopularity with villagers.

3. When you are out for day or evening, try to avoid carrying anything you don't need at the time. Hotels can keep your extra money, cameras, passport, and other valuables in their safes. In villages, I have left my tourist card and all extra money with the honest owner of the cabin I was using. A photocopy of the first several pages of your passport including its number, your photo, and your entry visa stamped at the airport are sufficient and should always be carried. That saved me when my wallet was stolen (from an outside pack pocket I should never have put it in) as the passport also had the visa stamped on it. Of course, passport and credit card numbers should be recorded and kept separately so you have them when reporting a theft. Lately, the police have stopped travelers on the street and demanded to see passports, but the photocopy seems to be acceptable as long as it includes your photo. Of course, if you plan to stay 30 days or less, you may have only a tourist card.

Costa Ricans carry nothing of value in pockets, even a cheap pen in a shirt pocket. Men should never carry anything in back pockets. For men or women once in the country, a traveler's pouch worn inside clothes is safer. Some have a loop that fits over a man's belt, allowing the pouch, big enough for a flat billfold, to hang down inside trousers. For women, it's best to avoid nylon zipped bags which seem to be targets, and instead use a purse with secure handles and a short shoulder strap that allows the purse to be carried under your upper arm. I have never had a problem carrying a briefcase, which has inner pockets and zips securely outside, but I have had a cloth bag unzipped on the street. There are utility leather handbags for $20 or less in Costa Rica that zip securely and are big enough to hold billfold, shopping bag, and even a camera. Friends who carry these have had no problems.

In summary, don't bring anything you don't really need, try not to carry anything you don't need that day, and watch or have someone else watch anything you put down. These precautions apply as well anywhere you travel and are not unique to Costa Rica.

Traveling With Children

Costa Rica is a fine place to bring children. Costa Ricans love them and welcome visitors with them. The cleanliness of food and water leave you few worries. There's lots for them to see and do. They'll pick up Spanish quickly if they play with local children. Readers who have traveled with infants note that

Girl in Uvita shows us her pet parrots.

62

disposable diapers are very expensive and not always available outside San Jose. They advise bringing all you'll need but say that will leave you lots of room in baggage going home for souvenirs and gifts. Restaurants often do have high chairs and booster seats, but car seats are not generally available. Milk in cartons which has been radiated so it doesn't have to be refrigerated until it's opened is in stores in any large town.

Children, even infants, need identification anytime they cross international borders. If they are under 18 and stay in Costa Rica more than 30 days, they require permission from the Patronato Office (c. 19, av. 6) to leave the country. Both parents must go to get it, or a single parent traveling alone must have the permission of the other notarized by the Costa Rican consul nearest the child's residence to show. A travel agent may be able to get the permission if you give him the child's passport and 2 extra passport photos.

Cultural Sensitivity

Nowhere in the world are people more helpful, hospitable and friendly than Costa Ricans. Most have had enough contact with North Americans (many have lived for years in the United States or elsewhere abroad) to be understanding and to forgive us our gringo differences. When I asked a young Costa Rican how he spoke such accent-free English, he said "Oh, I lived in Los Angeles for 15 years." He made some of the comments and suggestions given here.

Dress—San Jose is more cosmopolitan than elsewhere in the country and slacks on women are acceptable here. You will see young ticas in blue jeans frequently. Do dress up for performances at the National Theater and other occasions important to the Costa Ricans. Wearing blue jeans there doesn't show respect to the people or their culture. For men or women, shorts are for sports and the beach only. In villages which may be less liberal, I wear skirts unless I'm going hiking or riding.

All Latin Americans consider themselves as American as citizens of the United States of America. Travelers from the United States can show consideration, and it will be appreciated, if

Farmers sell fruits and vegetables in weekly street markets like this one in Santa Ana.

they refer to themselves as "norteamericanos" or North Americans.

Machismo still exists in Latin American, but much less in Costa Rica than elsewhere and is much less a problem for foreign women here than in most other places. The most obvious sign I have seen in all my rambling is polite surprise from men and women alike at the weird things gringo women do—travel alone, hike, ride, swim and live alone, fly planes, operate their own boats and businesses, and make all the important decisions in their own lives. When I was camping by myself in Santa Rosa National Park, the mother of a large family swarming around the campground asked, "are you a writer?". Apparently writers are forgiven for being even crazier than other tourists and wanting solitude. I have never had an incident involving a Costa Rican despite my often being the only woman present.

A Costa Rican advises, "Don't be blatant in manners, dress or voice. Blend in. The locals catch on quickly if you stand out. Explain clearly (not loudly) what you need and want. Check things said to you for truth." People sometimes want to please you enough to say "si", yes, to anything you ask. "Single North American girls have a bad reputation, so many men think they're an easy catch. Show that you respect yourself."

Nude bathing is at best completely offensive to Costa Ricans. At worst, it's downright dangerous to bathers in some areas and has led to serious incidents. The white sand beach at Cahuita may look like a deserted island to you, but it's these people's front yard and the path behind it through coconut palms is the walkway to their homes. In some coastal villages, the local girls are never taught to swim, though safety and enjoyment are lost because their parents don't want them exposed to nudity on the beach. What a shame!

Costa Rican men are polite and possibly more considerate than you are used to. One can be a lady or gentleman anywhere. Here you'll find that an interest in the people and their concerns makes your trip more enjoyable and enlightening.

How To Get There

Presently the recommended way to get to Costa Rica is by airline to San Jose with the exception of stopping through on a cruise ship for a day or perhaps of riding a bus north from Panama. Some people drive the Inter-American Highway or ride buses, with bus riding undoubtedly safer than driving your own vehicle. Until peace returns to Guatemala, El Salvador, and Nicaragua, driving through them isn't safe. If you ride the LACSA (Costa Rican) flight from Los Angeles or the SAHSA (Honduran) flight from New Orleans, you may be surprised to land at San Salvador or Managua briefly en route.

Do you want just a glimpse of Costa Rica now, and maybe plan to come back later for a longer visit? Each year more cruise ships, usually running between Mexico and the Panama Canal, stop for a day at the Pacific port of Caldera. Their passengers ride the electric train on part of its scenic route, have lunch in San Jose with tours of the National Theater and National Museum, do a bit of shopping, and visit Sarchí's oxcart factory before returning to their ship. It's a full day and a fine introduction to Costa Rica. The cruise lines stopping in Costa Rica include Regency Cruises, Royal Viking Lines, Bermuda Star Line, Cunard, Royal Cruises, Ocean Cruises, and Special Expeditions.

Cruise ship *Royal Odyssey* docked at Caldera while passengers visit San Jose.

For the lowest air fares, if you're going for 30 days or less, have your travel agent search carefully for excursion fares or "tour based" package plans which may involve some nights at designated hotels, but often take a large discount off the regular fare. There are many well-informed travel agents who are willing to make the effort. Space will not allow us to list them all, but we include 3 who are especially capable in organizing Costa Rican trips for any budget:

America's Tours & Travel
Javier Pinel
1402 Third Ave., Suite 1019
Seattle, WA 98101-3058
(800) 553-2513 in U.S.
(206) 623-8850 in WA

Preferred Adventures Ltd.
Karen L. Johnson, CTC
One West Water St., Suite 300
St. Paul, MN 55107
(612) 222-8131

Worldwide Holidays
Dolores Batchelor
7800 Red Rd., Suite 112
So. Miami, FL 33143
1-800-327-9854
(305) 665-0841 in FL

The following airlines fly to Costa Rica from Europe, North and South America: For their local addresses, see your travel agent. Their San Jose addresses are given because you'll need to confirm your return flight at least 72 hours before the flight.

AVIANCA/SAM
Ave. 52, Calle 1/3
Tel.22-97-94

PAN AMERICAN
Tel. 800-221-1111(U.S.)

COPA
Calle 1 Ave. 5
Tel. 22-49-07
Airport tel. 41-25-91

IBERIA
Calle 1 Ave 2/4
Tel 41-41-25

EASTERN
Paseo Colón
Tel. 22-56-55

KLM
Calle 1 Ave ctl/1
Tel. 21-09-22

LACSA
Hotel Torremolinos
Tel. 31-05-11
Airport tel 41-62-44

MEXICANA
Calle 1 Ave. 2/4
Tel. 22-17-11

SAHSA
Calle 1/3 Ave. 5
Tel. 21-57-74, 21-55-61

SANSA (local airline)
Calle 24 Ave. ctl/1
Tel. 21-94-14, 33-03-07

TACA
Calle 1, Ave. 3
Tel. 22-17-90, 22-17-44

Baggage. Most international airlines allow 66 lbs. of baggage. Some weigh your carry-on bag as part of it. You'll be happier if you don't have to carry or look after more than that anyway. SAHSA, for one, charges $1 per pound for excess baggage from New Orleans to San Jose! There's motivation for packing light!

Experienced travelers advise you to check your baggage only to your point of departure from your home country and make the transfer to the international airline yourself. It's much easier to cope with lost luggage in Miami than to wonder where it went after you arrive in San Jose. Your luggage should be secure, locked, and not easy to slit with a knife.

It should be well marked and have your address inside as well. I use laundry marking pen on the luggage itself as well as luggage tags. Your carry-on bag must fit under the seat in front of you. It should contain medicine and any other really indispensables—or irreplaceables. Mine has my address books, cameras, binoculars, film, glasses, bathing suit, and one set of clothes including shoes. Anything else I could replace in San Jose if I had to. Any prescription drugs should be in their original containers. You are allowed to take into Costa Rica $100 value in gifts for friends.

You may bring 2 cameras and any reasonable amount of film. If you are doing serious or professional photography and will need more than that you are advised to take a list of your equipment and serial numbers to the nearest Costa Rican consulate before you leave home. They simply want to be sure you will bring them back with you instead of selling them en route. If your equipment, including watch and binoculars, wasn't made in your home country, you may save some delay on your return by taking the same list and equipment to your own country's nearest customs office for recording (this list is then good for as long as you own the equipment and doesn't have to be redone for each trip).

International Flights

From Miami: **LACSA,** U.S. 1-800-225-2272; Canada & U.S. West Coast 1-800-663-2344

Pan American, U.S. and Canada 1-800-221-1111 **Eastern,** U.S. 1-800-327-8376

Also **TACA,** 1-800-535-8780, and **TAN.**

From New York: **LACSA.** From New Orleans: **LACSA, SAHSA,** 1-800-327-1225, **TACA.**

From Houston: **TACA, SAHSA.**

From Los Angeles: **LACSA, Mexicana**, 1-800-531-7923 (U.S.),
TACA.

From San Francisco: **Pan American, Mexicana.** Other connections can be made in Mexico City. **KLM,** 1-800-556-777, (U.S. & Canada) and **Iberia,** 1-800-221-9741 (U.S.), fly from Europe to Costa Rica.

I have been told that flying from Canada to Costa Rica is often cheaper if one starts from inside the U. S. than from within Canada.

Domestic Flights:

SANSA To/From: Quepos,   Rió Frió. Coto 47, Golfito, Liberia, Tamarindo .

SANSA's classic DC-3 takes off from Juan Santamaria.

Entry & Departure Requirements

While the documentation and procedures vary somewhat depending on your citizenship, the requirements for U.S. and Canadian citizens given here are typical. To encourage tourism, the entry and exit procedures were greatly streamlined in 1989.

While having a current passport is recommended and makes your travels more flexible, for visits of 30 days or less, you don't need one. You do need at least two pieces of identification, preferably with your photo on at least one of them, such as driver's license, birth certificate, voting registration, and even an expired passport. You will have to buy a tourist card (about $2) at the airline desk at your point of departure from the United States, or at the Immigration desk in the San Jose airport. This is your 30 day visa and cannot be extended.

If you have a current passport, a 90 day visa will be stamped into it, and you won't need extentions or an exit visa to stay in Costa Rica for 90 days! At the end of 90 days you will need to leave Costa Rica for at least 72 hours. You will need to show a round trip or "onward" ticket showing that you have means of leaving Costa Rica.

If you are traveling with minor children, including infants, they will need to have identification, including pictures. Passports are recommended. If only one parent is traveling with the child(ren), you will need permission from the other parent, both to enter and leave Costa Rica with them, notarized, and stamped by the Costa Rican consul nearest your home.

You should carry your passport or tourist card with you, as the police have the right to ask you to show it at any time. Many experienced travelers, including this one, make a photocopy of the first 3 pages of the passport showing the photo and the visa stamp, and carry that on the street instead of the whole passport. The passport is needed when renting a car or cashing travelers' checks.

This space is not a mistake! It shows you how much red tape the Costa Rican government cut for tourists when it extended the initial visa from 30 days to 90 with a passport! I was able to eliminate the complicated explanation of extending your stay that filled this space. Long live the Costa Ricans responsible for this simplification!

Entering Costa Rica

Costa Rica has made entry at the airport as simple and convenient as I've ever seen it. You line up before Immigration's windows just inside the terminal and they check your passport and look in the big book of computer records to see if you've been in trouble here before. If you haven't, you're quickly allowed on past the offices for exchanging money or cashing travelers' checks into colones, and the ICT office which can call hotels downtown to find a room for you. If you use either of these services, your baggage will already be waiting for you in the claim area when you get there. Customs check of your baggage is quick and efficient (perhaps more detailed if you come from cocaine growing countries to the south), and 20 minutes from the time you entered the terminal, you may be climbing the stairs to the street outside! Welcome to Costa Rica!

Outside you'll find cabs, minibuses, car rentals and the bus stop for the San Jose-Alajuela bus just across the driveway. The latter is only a few cents all the way to San Jose, but won't take any more than carry-on luggage. It's worth remembering if you ever turn in a rental car at the airport. With tourist luggage, the cheapest way to town is the minibus which will stop at hotels. Airport cabs cost about twice as much per mile as all other cabs in the country and they won't bargain. It's about $8 to town by cab. Enjoy the ride to San Jose on the modern "autopista", turnpike, past coffee plantations, several industrial plants. Hospital Mexico, several deluxe hotels, and the Cariari Country Club. You'll pass Sabana Park as you enter downtown San Jose.

What to Bring

You'll undoubtedly have some items you'd add to this list, but keep it light and leave room for what you may want to bring back. If you select 1 or 2 base colors and make sure everything else goes with them, you'll have a variety of costumes with a limited wardrobe. Cotton is cooler than synthetics, but everything should be wash and wear. I never travel with light-colored slacks, shorts, or skirts as they look grubby after I've sat down twice. I bring a navy lightweight suit with shirt and slacks, a navy denim skirt, field pants and hiking shorts. All blouses are in light colors that go with them. Navy Birkenstock sandals softened the miles of San Jose's stone sidewalks and worked well with a denim skirt for days at a time in buses and jeeps in the countryside. A skirt is far cooler on the coasts than slacks, and should be full enough to allow climbing into bus or boat.

Men should bring a lightweight suit and 1 or 2 ties (for travel and evening in San Jose), plus slacks. As soon as possible, you'll want a guayabera shirt, the white or cream shirt Latin American men wear open at the neck and not tucked in. It's dressy enough for almost anything and saves wearing ties, etc. to dinner. You don't need coat and tie outside of San Jose. Flowered shirts from Hawaii will mark you a tourist and are suitable only at the beach.

Women:
1 suit w/skirt & slacks
skirts (1 denim, 1 print, etc.)
3 blouses (capped or short
  sleeves)

1 dressy dress
1 pair slacks
1 pair walking shorts
1 bathing suit
Sweater or light jacket
3 sets underwear
3 pairs socks, 2 pairs
  pantyhose
1 pair street shoes (walking)
2 pairs sandals (1 pair each,
1 pair running or tennis shoes
Manicure set, inexpensive
  earrings

Men:
1 suit
2 dress shirts

3 sport shirts
2 pairs slacks
1 pair jeans or equiv.
1 pair walking shorts
1 pair swimming trunks
Sweater or sport jacket
  3 sets underwear
4 pairs socks
1 pair street shoes
1 pair sandals
1 pair running or tennis shoes
Shaving gear

Both Men and Women
Towel (hotels won't let theirs
  go to the beach)
Washcloth
Universal flat drain cover for
  wash basin
Sun hat
Sun glasses
Toilet paper (small amount)
Sunscreen (SPF #4 or 6 and
  SPF #15 or 18)
Insect repellent
Anti-itch ointment
Bandaids
Moleskin
Aspirin
Kaopectate
Pepto Bismol
Toothbrush, paste, cup

Ear plugs (if you can sleep with
  them)
Sewing kit
Alarm clock
Flashlight
Plastic bags, clothespins & line
According to your special
  interests:
Fins, mask snorkel
Day pack
Sleeping or bivouac bag
Canteen & water drops
Pocket knife
Cup, spoon, bowl
Binoculars
Photograph gear
Battery-powered fan
Hiking boots
Goretex parka, pants

Hairbrush & comb
Vitamin pills (optional)
Umbrella, folding. Cheap in
   San Jose. Essential.

Pile jacket
Stocking cap

If you plan to spend many nights in the discos of San Jose, or you're a field biologist or in the Peace Corps, your interests will affect your choices.

Time

Costa Rica is on Central Standard Time, 6 hours behind Greenwich Mean Time. Since it's as far east as Miami, in the Eastern Time Zone, the sun comes up around 6 a.m. all year and sets in early evening. The whole country seems to get an early start to its day.

Telephones

You can dial direct between Costa Rica and most other countries, keeping track of time zones. It's more expensive to dial from Costa Rica to the U.S. than in the other direction, especially if you use the low cost times of day. The access numbers for Costa Rica are 011-506 plus the number. From Costa Rica to the U.S. dial 116 plus the number. Within Costa Rica there are some villages with just 1 phone number with or without an exchange and extension, e.g. Cahuita and Puerto Viejo. Many hotels on the coasts do have a San Jose number. This can be the easiest way to make reservations for lower-priced hotels which don't have foreign representatives. Generally, if you want reservations in hotels that cost less than $12/night, you'll need to speak Spanish.

Pay phones in San Jose seem to be on busy corners with loud diesel trucks shifting gears. Costa Rican coins come in old, new, and newer denominations, and the phone you're facing usually takes coins you don't have. More now take the new 2 colon piece so it's worth saving these. Passersby will help if they can. Use their help or find a phone inside somewhere. There's a pay phone just outside the ICT office under the Cultural Plaza, generally a quiet spot.

Many foreigners who've moved into Costa Rica haven't been able to get phones in their own names so the phones are listed in someone else's, effectively making them unlisted. Be sure

Las Brisas del Pacifico at Sámara.

you have your friends' numbers as you won't be able to look them up.

For international calls, you can dial direct from private phones. For an English-speaking operator, dial 116. To call to Canada or the United Staes, dial 001, 116, the area code and number. You can use the international number on your phone credit card. In San Jose, the Radiográfica, at c. 1, av. 5 is open from 7 a.m. to 10 p.m. From it you can wire or telephone another country, with English-speaking assistance if you need it. Unfortunately the phone on the busy corner outside is the one to use for calls within Costa Rica.

Addresses

Practically all Costa Rican mailing addresses are "Apartados," abbreviated "Apdo.", meaning post office box. Street numbers don't exist or aren't used. Neither are street names outside of San Jose. All directions are given in meters or varas (33 inches) from something else which may not still be there. The tree was cut down or the Coca Cola bottling plant is long gone, but everyone knows where it was! I lived in a very nice house in

75

a good suburb of San Jose, but the address was (in Spanish, of course) "225 meters south and 100 meters west of the church, near the brown garbage container." Don't try it in the dark the first time, especially from a bus and bus stop you don't know. A taxi driver might be able to find it. A friend who had to pick me up was smart enough to ask whether those directions were from the front or back of the big church. You may want a compass as well as some patience.

Mail

Air mail takes about 5 days each way between Costa Rica and the U.S. or Canada, the same to Europe. Surface mail takes weeks. If you're sending mail from Costa Rica, mail it at your hotel desk or a main post office, for reliability, and don't put anything but a letter in it. Mail to you should be sent in care of your hotel or to you at "Lista De Correos," general delivery. Zip or postal codes are put before the name of the town, e.g. 1000 San Jose. Do underline both Costa Rica and Central America on the envelope, in hopes the postal clerks won't send it to Puerto Rico!

Try not to have anyone send you anything but letters. A few personal photographs in a standard letter envelope do seem to go directly through the mail. Other items go to customs warehouses, often in another town, and the duty can be very high, with no relation to the value of the item. Getting there at the right time to pick it up can be a big nuisance. Even cassette tapes with messages on them aren't worth it. The same applies to packages you might want to send Costa Rican friends after you get home. Don't do it. They might have to pay $15 in duty and spend half a day to pick up a $5 present. Perhaps you can find a friend visiting Costa Rica who won't mind taking something small in the $100 in gifts a traveler can bring.

Getting Around

Public transportation within the country is subsidized and is very reasonable.

Air SANSA is the airline within Costa Rica with daily (or at least several times weekly) flights between San Jose and Liberia, Tamarindo, Quepos, Golfito, and Coto 47 near the Panamanian border. Most fares are under $20, and the flights are about half an hour.

Trains We've discussed the train to Limón and the electric train to Puntarenas, both recommended scenic rides at minimal cost. The Northern Railway which runs to Limón also has shorter runs to Alajuela and Heredia. Check with the train station at Ave. 3 Calle 17/19 or the ICT for schedules. In San Jose, while the tracks connect the two stations, the station for the Pacific train is in the southwest corner of town at Ave. 20 Calle 2. The Pacific train leaves several times a day.

Oxcarts work everywhere in the country and haul anything.

Buses Costa Ricans ride buses to go anywhere. If there's a road, there's probably a bus, though it may not be daily. Buses on main highways to Golfito, Puerto Limón, Puntarenas, and Liberia are very comfortable. Fares are low—$3 will take you a long distance. The bus from San Jose to Golfito takes about 7 hours, including a lunch stop, and follows the Inter-American Highway from Cartago south over the summit of Cerro de la Muerte, over 11,000 ft. If it's clear, you have glimpses of both the Atlantic and Pacific Oceans as the road winds along the backbone of the Talamanca Range. It drops down to the Valle de General across a slope where landslides during the rainy season sometimes do block it and reaches Golfito in mid-afternoon, for about $3.75 U.S.!

Buses in San Jose cost only a few colones, usually less than a dime. Often 15 or 20 cents in colones is the fare for a half hour ride in from the suburbs. It's a good use for the small change you accumulate. Most of the buses to suburbs start at or pass close by the "Coca Cola", site of the long-gone Coca Cola bottling plant at Ave. 1 and Calle 16. It's a rough neighborhood, best avoided at night and a place to be careful by day. From here you can get buses to Ciudad Colón, Santa Ana, Escazú, Sarchí, and Naranjo, as well as Quepos and Orotina. Nearby are stops for most areas west of San Jose, including Guanacaste. Other bus terminals or stops in San Jose are as follows:

Alajuela: Ave. 2, Calle 14
Cañas: Calle 16, Ave. 1/3
Cartago, Turrialba: Calle 13, Ave. Ctl./2
Golfito: Ave. 18, Calle 4 (near Pacific RR)
Guápiles: Calle 12, Ave. 7/9
Liberia: Calle 14, Ave. 1/3 (near Coca Cola)
Limón: Ave. 3, Calle 19/21 (near Atlantic RR)
Nicoya: Calle 14, Ave. 5 (near Coca Cola)
Puerto Viejo de Sarapiqui (La Selva area): Calle 12, Ave. 7/9
Puntarenas: Calle 12, Ave. 7/9 (near Coca Cola)
San Isidro: Calle 15, Ave. 7/9
Santa Cruz: Calle 16, Ave. 1/3 (near Coca Cola)
Tilarán: Calle 12, Ave. 9/11.
Zarcero: Calle 16, Ave. 3 (near Coca Cola)
Zona Sur: Ave. 11, Calle 4.

Even for suburban buses, your best chance of having a seat is to catch the bus at the Coca Cola terminal instead of at one of its later stops. For buses going farther, it's best to get the ticket the day before (especially for weekends or holidays) and get there an hour early. Buses run from early morning until 10 or 11 at night, so you often have no choice but taxis after theater or dinner with friends. Taxis at such hours don't bargain easily, but sometimes you can share. In other areas, such as Quepos and Manuel Antonio, the buses stop much earlier and you are reduced to taxis.

Nicaragua: SIRCA bus to Managua, 12 hours, starting at 5:30 a.m. from Calle 11, Ave. 2. There's also a local bus to the border at Peñas Blancas, but you have to walk 4 km. to catch the bus on the other side. A visa is not required for US citizens (I'd call 33-87-47 and check on this for latest info), but you are required to change at least $60 in US dollars at the official rate at the border.

Panama: Passport and visa required, plus a return or onward ticket. TICA Bus, Calle 9, Ave. 4, runs daily to Panama City. TRACOPA bus, Ave. 18, Calle 4, runs to David, Panama, and you take another bus to Panama City.

Airlines also fly direct from San Jose to both capitals. Note that you'll need an exit visa from Costa Rica if you've been in the country for more than 30 days.

If you're going to ride buses often, some Spanish is essential for at least one member of your party. You do have to be able to ask and receive directions and schedules. Around tourist hotels, someone always speaks English. In and around public buses they don't necessarily. You don't need very much, however, if you're polite and prepared for some confusion. Be careful of your possessions, especially around the San Jose stations, and don't show much money when buying tickets. Try to carry as little luggage as possible. Some buses have storage below, but local buses don't, and backpacks or large suitcases don't fit on the overhead racks inside.

4-wheel drive taxis in Tilaran tell you about surrounding roads.

Taxis Taxis are quite inexpensive, except for the airport cabs, which charge double. The San Jose cabs have meters, called "marias", but many drivers refuse to turn them on. Fares are a matter of bargaining—the more Spanish, the better. You should agree on the fare before getting into the cab. Fares can vary according to the time of day, the driver's attitude, yours, how

79

affluent you look (don't expect to bargain about 30 colones with a Nikon hanging around you neck!), and whether you're going or coming from an expensive hotel. My mail was held at a friend's office in the Playboy Hotel. I soon learned to save 40 colones every trip by naming the nearest street intersection instead of the hotel when agreeing on the fare, though I could later direct the cab to the door.

You can ask several drivers to reach a consensus. Some hotel desks are good sources of advice, while those at deluxe hotels may add a bit. The ICT office under the Cultural Plaza may tell you the going rate is something like 40 colones for the first kilometer and 12 for each additional. Our San Jose street map shows kilometers so you can calculate what the fare should be. If the driver won't use his meter within the city, you can note his permit number and car license for the Ministry of Public Transport complaint forms which the ICT information office has. The meters will only read to 15 kilometers, so if you're going farther, you'll have to bargain.

In outlying areas some cabs are 4-wheel drive. Particularly if there are several in your party, it may be practical to hire a cab and driver for the day for some trips, e.g. from Puerto Limón to Cahuita or Puerto Viejo and back. They'll add a bit for the state of the road, but it may save you hours of waiting for a bus to come back. Taxi drivers are not tipped.

Tours Tours are increasing throughout Costa Rica, although practically all are still based in San Jose. There are multi-day tours to the more remote national parks, Barra Colorado, Tortuguero, Monteverde, and the Nicoya Peninsula. There are many day tours in and around San Jose, mostly in minivans. They pick you up and drop you off at your hotel, and you may be able to visit several sites in one day, e.g. Irazú and the Orosi Valley. The driver speaks English and any other languages required. He'll tell you about what you're passing en route to the main object. You spend your time sightseeing instead of waiting in bus stations or perhaps riding crowded buses, and the vans are clean and comfortable. You pay for the extra service and you don't meet Costa Ricans except for your driver. Tour drivers are tipped.

80

The tours I have been on have been excellent, even to places I have also reached by public bus such as Irazú and Poás. There are nature and other special interest tours. The One Day Adventure Tours are a cooperative effort by Calypso Tours, with boat tours in the Gulf of Nicoya, and Costa Rica Expeditions, rafting on the Reventazón River. All of them are well done and fun.

Tours on the train use the newly refurbished cars with comfortable seats, restaurant and bar. The tour operators who contributed to that cost have priority in reserving the space which may or may not be available to the independent traveler. More tours and operators are being added to the list you'll find at the back of this book.

Car rental This isn't something to jump into as lightly as you might at home. Costa Rica has one of the world's highest per capita accident rates. Passing on the narrow two-lane (or less) roads is a very macho competitive sport. Try Sunday afternoon on the highway above Esparza with the crowd returning from a weekend at the beach competing with buses and loaded cattle trucks heading for Monday market in San Jose. On the winding, steep grades buses and trucks pass in both directions. San Jose streets are one-way and narrow with almost no parking except lots and garages.

There are freeways for some miles near San Jose. Cars shouldn't be left overnight except in a fenced area. In daylight all baggage should be stowed out of sight in the trunk. I can think of few things that would persuade me to drive in San Jose at all. Cars in Costa Rica don't have heaters or defrosters, though the controls may be there. You don't need heaters, but do need defrosters in the rain (you need a rag to wipe with). Prices for rentals are similar to those in the United States, though gas is over $2 U.S. per gallon. International rental chains will take major credit cards.

Your valid driver's license is good for 3 months in Costa Rica. After that you need to get one there. Insurance is a state monopoly and you can get it through the car rental agency. Rental agencies in the San Jose area are listed below. Note that most are on the west side of downtown San Jose or at the airport, or both.

For a higher rate, some have 4-wheel drive vehicles. Be sure that's what you need before spending the extra money for a vehicle that's less comfortable for any number of people over two. Most of the popular beaches can be reached by ordinary cars. Ask about road conditions. Cars can be rented with air conditioning, but you should check to be sure it really cools the air rather than just blowing it.

If you're spending a week at a resort, it may not make sense to have a rental car parked there costing money when there's usually some cheaper, less worrisome way to get there. However, if there's a group of you with limited time, it can be a good solution.

I rented the smallest possible Toyota from Budget for a 4-day research swing through Jacó Beach, Quepos and Manuel Antonio, Punta Dominical, and Golfito, and back to San Jose. I couldn't have covered the ground with all the stops I needed any other way. Everything went well. The car cost $180 U.S. including the fuel I bought. Without the unlimited mileage I needed, 4 days' rental would be much cheaper.

Car Rental Agencies

Accion Rent a Car
Sabana Norte

Phone 32-96-37

Avis Rent a Car
Calle 36, Ave. 7
Phone 22-60-66

Budget Rent a Car
Calle 30, Paseo Colón
Phone 23-32-84

Dollar Rent a Car
Calle ctl., Ave. 9
Phone 33-33-39

El Indio Rent a Car
Calle 40/42, Ave. ctl.
Phone 33-21-57

Elegante Rent a Car
Calle 10, Ave. 13/15
or Calle 24, Ave. 5/7
Phone 21-01-36

National Car Rental
Calle 30, Paso Colón
Phone 33-44-06

Tico Rent A Car, S.A.
Calle 10, Ave. 13/15
Phone 21-01-36

Toyota Rent a Car
Calle 36, Ave. 7
Phone 23-22-50

Global Rent-A Car
Ave. 7, Calle 7/9
Phone 23-53-25

Take it easy on the 10 km of bad road around Lake Arenal.

4-wheel drive taxi between Uvita and Punta Dominical.

If you do have an accident, don't move the vehicles until the police make out a report. Note the traffic police numbers below.

Traffic Police

San Jose	22-43-05, 23-80-45, 22-10-05
Alajuela	41-62-08
Cartago	51-90-64
Heredia	37-04-38
Liberia	66-04-09
Limón	58-11-48
Puntarenas	61-03-40

Driving in Costa Rica requires more concentration than I usually give it at home, even on the freeways near San Jose. On the back roads, you are advised to "drive like a bullfighter," as one friend said, demonstrating how he passed around holes in the road. Save wear and tear on vehicle and passengers by slowing and shifting as necessary for bumps. Unlit livestock, holes, and pedestrians make driving at night something to avoid. If you find fresh branches lying in the road, it means someone has car trouble just ahead.

Service stations are far apart, and many villages have none. You should fill up in main towns like Liberia, Santa Cruz, or Nicoya before heading to beach resorts. These also may be the only places you can get tire or other repairs.

Hitchhiking On back roads, you'll meet people trying to get a ride to town because there isn't a bus until tomorrow or the next day. I'm not sure how successful they are on roads with little traffic, but you may not be able to count on it anywhere in the country. With bus fare so cheap, that's the way to go if there's a bus. Otherwise, it's worth asking and trying to find someone going the same way.

Maps Maps to help you get around are free or inexpensive everywhere. ICT and your hotel can furnish maps of downtown San Jose and simple resort maps of the country. Car rental agencies give out road maps, though no one seems to have one with most of the smaller roads, and of course none tells you which streams have bridges. The stationers/bookstores, Libreria Lehmann, Ave. ctl, Calle 1/3, and Libreria Universal, Ave. ctl, Calle ctl/1, have good map sections. At Lehmann's, I found the aeronautical chart of Costa Rica. At a scale of 1:500,000, it's a great map to bring back to show your friends where you've been as it shows all the mountains in shaded relief so you can see the shape of the country. It's about 2½ by 3½ feet, a fine, inexpensive souvenir. They also have smaller maps that show just about anything. The Ministry of Transport, Ave. 18, Calle 9, has topographic maps and street maps of towns.

Hotel Comments

Hotels in each town are described as I found them, either on inspection or by staying in them. Some, inspected at quiet midday, may prove to have a cantina operating loudly at night in the block behind. A change of owner or manager could make a large difference for better or worse in cleanliness or service. I welcome comments based on your experience.

Costa Rica has over 300 hotels, some luxurious and some basic where farm workers stay when they come to town on weekends. In between are many inexpensive to moderate hotels with very considerate staffs. You can decide not only what you're willing to pay, but how much luxury you want. Do you want to stay in a "tipico" hotel, where you feel the character of the country and some of your fellow residents are Costa Rican, or do you want to relax in the same atmosphere you'd find in Hawaii or Palm Springs? Or would you like some of each for variety?

Our recommendation is given carefully, knowing how much management can change. A hotel listed as recommended is not only clean and attractive, but has a very **hospitable** staff and represents an exceptional value in its price range. It may not be the most luxurious hotel in the area. If you want more facilities or service, it may not be the one you would choose. Our tastes vary.

For this book, we inspected (with a checklist) over 200 hotels all over the country, priced from $.75 to $150 per night, single. We looked at almost all the moderate to luxurious hotels. However, when we found clean hotels in good neighborhoods for less than $3 single, we felt we could do more for you than spend days wandering through the red light districts of San Jose and Puerto Limón inspecting the cheap ones there. If you want these, many are listed in the *The South America Handbook* and

85

South America On a Shoestring chapter, on Costa Rica.

Costa Rica has many small hotels with a dozen rooms or less, often far from major towns. Most hotels in San Jose or the surrounding hills don't have air conditioning as it's cool at that altitude. On the coasts, most travelers from temperate climates will want at least a fan or a building that is built to catch every breeze. On the coast, many inexpensive places don't have hot water, but the tap water is lukewarm. Hotels rated inexpensive and higher generally will cash travelers' checks though the exchange rate may not be as good as the bank's, but it's a real help when there is no bank in a resort town. They will often take major credit cards. Some of them have reservation agents abroad whom your travel agent can call free. Without these, you'll have to make your own reservations or get help from the ICT office in the airport when you arrive (they called for me and made the reservations before I cleared customs). The hotels generally have someone behind the desk who speaks English. Often there are local tour representatives in the lobby with whom you can book sightseeing tours.

In less expensive hotels, you're likely to be more on your own if your Spanish is limited, though the manager will often go to amazing lengths to help you. On the East Coast practically all the blacks speak English. You may have a choice between rooms with and without bath. You should inspect rooms in really basic hotels before checking in to see if they're what you want. Everyone has his own definition of basic.

If you make reservations, you should make every effort to keep them or to cancel well ahead. A hotel with very few rooms may have turned away business to hold your reservation, put on extra staff, or laid in more food. This is expecially important for groups, but should be done by individuals as well.

The hotels are listed for each town later in this book. The exchange rate at the time was 75 colones/$1 U.S. Since then, the colon has been devalued slightly and is expected to drop further. Expensive hotels give their prices in dollars which they don't decrease with changes in the exchange rate. None of the prices here include the 13% tourist and sales tax charged nationally or any service charge. Inflation will cause some rates to rise, but probably not greatly as long as tourism is depressed

De Paso manager and author beside hotel's pool.

due to tensions in the nations north of Costa Rica. Some hotels have no rate for singles and simply charge a rate for the room. Some coastal hotels include meals with the rate, and may have a high season rate for December through March. These ranges are based on the minimum charge for singles and prices go higher for deluxe features. For the current exchange rate when you travel, you can call the nearest Costa Rican embassy or consulate or call the ICT office in Miami toll-free from the continental U.S., 1-800-327-7033.

Luxury	Over	$75/day	Range A+
Deluxe		$52-75	A
Expensive		$36-52	B
Moderate		$24-36	C
Inexpensive		$14-24	D
Budget		$8-14	E
Basic		up to $8	F

This scale refers to price for a single room in U.S. dollars only and does not refer to features of the hotel which may include a swimming pool in the budget range. A room or cabin for 4 may be a real bargain for a group or family even if it's not for a single.

Couples should ask for their preference in twin or double beds when making reservations. Hotels often have rooms with either. Many budget hotels have some rooms with bath and some without. Beach hotels often have some rooms with air conditioning and some with fans. In San Jose and at higher elevations you don't need it, but down on the coasts you probably will need a fan. Fan or generator noise can make earplugs welcome.

"Apartotels" and "cabinas" are terms you'll see often. An apartotel has rooms with kitchen facilities, often suites, and usually has weekly and monthly as well as daily rates. There are several in the San Jose area and a few elsewhere. They can be economical for families and very convenient if one is following a diet. "Cabina" means cabin but is used very loosely by the owners and occasionally even means a room in a multi-story building. Usually, if not cabin, it refers to motel-style ground level rooms. A "pension" is an inexpensive to basic hotel which usually does not serve meals even if it formerly did.

El Portico.

Camping

Camping at beaches and national parks is a practical way to stay. Sometimes the nearest hotel is 40 miles away. There are few commercial camping areas, e.g. Jacó Beach south end, and others where it's acceptable as long as you're not in someone's yard or field without permission. If you're camping high in the mountains, as on Rincon de la Vieja, you'll need a good sleeping bag and tent, though sometimes there are shelters or huts. For low-altitude camping here in the tropics, I've found my 18-ounce bivouac bag with a foam sleeping pad works. In rain, I'd want a plastic sheet overhead. The bivouac bag zips closed with a bug net panel, and I think I could sleep on any ant hill. However, a tent is more comfortable in heat than being zipped into a bag. Avoid grassy stock pastures, which often have chiggers and ticks.

I used the grassy, tree-shaded campground at Santa Rosa park two nights. The first night I was concerned about crawling creatures and tried sleeping on a picnic table. Unfortunately, it had a loose plank on one side and at midnight, it dumped me. Falling off a table while zipped up in a bivvy bag is a very helpless feeling! Peace ended at 4 a.m. when a family of howler monkeys on one side of camp joined a chorus of coyotes in the next field.

A hammock is the ideal tropical camp bed for those whose backs will tolerate one.

Camping is the only way to be on hand for turtle nesting or hatching on west coast beaches, and in such unpopulated places, keeping supplied with food and reliable water is your only concern. In settled areas, such as Manuel Antonio, camping is beautiful except during holiday crowds. There are more camping areas being added at beaches like Jacó and at Moin on the Caribbean.

Watching your gear or finding someone else to watch it is a problem if you're alone or in a small group and want to leave camp. At Manuel Antonio, the ranger station does keep gear for people. I've sometimes stayed in a hotel or cabina simply to have a place to leave gear. Often your best bet is to camp with others so someone is always in the area. Putting your name with permanent laundry marker on your gear to destroy its resale value may help.

There are RV parks along the Inter-American Highway and near San Jose and Heredia. When driving down the highway to Costa Rica again becomes safe, I'll go into detail on them in later editions.

Corvina, sea bass is on every menu. This Montezuma boy holds one fresh-caught.

Food

While I've met travelers who can remember after two weeks in New Guinea which night the meat was tough, I'm not one of them. If food is one of your real interests as a traveler, you'll have have fun exploring the well-advertised restaurants of every nation in San Jose. For inexpensive meals, small places called *sodas* will serve good plain food for a dollar or so for lunch. The best ice cream in Costa Rica is at the Pops chain. *Refrescos* are delightful drinks made with tropical fruits such as mangos and papayas blended with water or milk. *Gallo pinto* is a rice and bean dish that Costa Ricans eat for breakfast and at other meals as well. Shrimp and fish dishes are excellent. You'll find corvina, sea bass, cooked many tasty ways. *Langosta* (lobster) is expensive compared to other entrees, but very reasonable in beach areas where they're caught the same day. Steak is good, though grass-fed and lean, and very inexpensive.

In coastal heat, I especially enjoy fruit salads and *ceviche*, a cool fish cocktail made with corvina pickeled in lemon juice and seasoning. The best recipe I've eaten follows, courtesy of Yolanda Kaye and Martha Thomas at Costa Rica Expeditions:

Ceviche Recipe, Serves 6.

Fresh sea bass	1 kilo
Coriander (fresh if possible)	1 bunch
Sweet red peppers	2 medium
Onion	1 large
Garlic	3 cloves
Lemons	6-8 medium
Worcestershire sauce	½ t
Salt & pepper to taste	

Cut up sea bass   (or any firm-fleshed white fish such as sole, snapper, halibut, shark) into ½" cubes and place in non-metallic container. Finely chop coriander, peppers, onion, and garlic and mix with fish. Peel and wash the lemons. Then cut in half to juice. Peeling is very important as the oil in the skin will cause the ceviche to be bitter. You need enough lemon juice to cover the fish. Add worcestershire sauce, salt and pepper. Cover and refrigerate overnight at least.

Hotels where I've enjoyed the food will be mentioned in their individual comments. Restaurants noted are excellent, cheap and in places you might not easily find, one near Manuel Antonio and one in Santa Cruz. For the environmentally conscious, a note—tortuga (sea turtle) eggs are served in some bars, and the meat is served in restaurants in Limón. All species are endangered and taking eggs or meat is illegal in most places. It probably will continue as long as people maintain the market by buying them.

Health

Costa Rica is the cleanest, most healthful, tropical country I've visited. The people and government are concerned about health and have spent heavily on water supplies, hospitals, and health programs. You can safely drink the water in San Jose and all other major towns, as well as all licensed tourist hotels in outlying areas. In really basic places with their own wells or at roadside pulperias, you may want to stick to soda drinks from the bottle, etc. Late in the dry season, February through April, some outlying towns have water problems and you should not drink or brush teeth in it unless you are sure it's OK. I carry and use water purification drops when I'm refilling my canteen from streams or wells on camping trips.

Food. Milk is pasteurized and market stalls in community markets are incredibly clean. Fish stalls in San Jose, 70 plus miles from the sea, don't even smell fishy! In choosing restaurants, I don't take any more care than I would traveling in the U.S., and I have rarely been sick despite eating in a wide variety of places all over the country. If you buy fried food from streetside stalls or vendors on buses and trains, or eat salads in doubtful-looking places, you're on your own. Washing your hands and the pocket knife you may be using to peel fruit before eating is important.

Hikers and campers will probably want to bring insect repellent, though I have only used it a few times in Costa Rica. Note that "deet", the active ingredient in many repellents, makes many people more sensitive to sun. You can use Avon bath oil instead! If you walk across lowland cattle pastures you may encounter chiggers, an almost invisible mite, also found in the southern U.S., whose bite raises welts with a fierce itch that lasts some days. Staying on trails and roads is the best prevention. Being completely covered around the ankles, etc. and changing clothes immediately afterward helps. Sulfur powder dusted on socks and pants helps. It's worth carrying a soothing anti-itch lotion. Some people take an antihistamine before bedtime to reduce swelling and itching if they've been bitten.

If you camp or stay in primitive quarters, it's best to hang up all clothing and shake out shoes and clothes before putting them on.

In Belen's park, on the road to Playa Tamarindo, these women make super frescos.

Snakes Except for the Arctic, most areas of the world have poisonous snakes. Despite looking carefully anytime I step off a trail or put my hand up to a tree, I have only seen one poisonous snake outside the laboratory in Costa Rica (the non-poisonous boa constrictor in a national park doesn't count). However, I will keep looking for the fer-de-lance (called terciapelo or velvet snake here) which is highly poisonous and very aggressive, the coral snake, and bushmaster. Except for the coral snake, most are **very** well-camouflaged. In urban areas they aren't a problem. In rural places or wilderness, watch where you are walking, and avoid stream banks at night. If you want to see them safely, visit the snake lab in Coronado, a northeastern suburb of San Jose, and watch them milked for venom Friday afternoons at 1:30, from behind a plate glass window. The lab is open, free, weekday afternoons from 1 to 4, with live snakes of each kind displayed.

Medical Care. Costa Rica has excellent doctors and hospitals, with the majority in the San Jose area. All hospitals have English-speaking staff members and many doctors have trained in the U.S. or England. For emergency care, go to the hospitals or clinics. For other care, your consulate can provide a list of private doctors. Check with your health insurance before you leave home to see if you need additional coverage or forms.

Because costs are much lower and skills are high, many people from abroad come to Costa Rica for plastic surgery (especially face lifts), cataract operations, sessions at health spas, dental work, etc. A nursing home specializing in long term care for Alzheimer's patients recently opened.

Immunizations. Officially there are none required or listed as recommended for Costa Rica. If you're staying in major hotels and not camping out or snorkeling, that's fine. If you will be hiking or camping, or spending time near Costa Rica's borders which might not be recognized as barriers by germs and mosquitoes, you may want to take some of the precautions you would for other tropical areas. A gamma globulin shot makes you more resistant to many viruses, including hepatitis, for up to 6 months. Tetanus is a good shot for any outdoor person to keep current. Costa Rica eliminated malaria some years ago, but refugees have recently arrived with some cases. A weekly pill prescribed by your doctor to be taken for several weeks before, during, and after the trip is simple to take if you will be near the borders or going to any other tropical countries on the same trip. No immunizations are required for entry to the United States. Carrying a copy of your immunization records and prescriptions is sensible when traveling.

Sunburn. Ten degrees north of the equator, the sun's effect on unprotected skin is serious. A burn from one day in the sun can spoil the next several days of your trip. Long-term exposure can, besides giving you a tan, age your skin drastically. I don't think the leather look has improved the appearance of anyone since Sitting Bull. Fortunately, you can avoid this and still go home with a healthy glow.

Using shade where available, a sunscreen lotion, a sun hat, and discretion with the midday sun and length of exposure are sensible. Here you will tan through a thin shirt or while lying in the shade near a beach. I wear a long-sleeved shirt and long pants anytime I'm riding horses or open boats. Bring effective sunscreens containing PABA. They are labeled now with sun protection factors (SPF), supposed to indicate how much longer

Poolside at Jaco Beach Hotel.

an average person can stay out without burning. You will **not** be in average conditions. As a blonde who does tan well, I use creams with an SPF of 4 or 6 for daytime moisturizers even in the Central Valley. On the beach or outdoors, I use gels with SPFs of 15 to 20, the highest generally available. These have names like Block Out and Total Eclipse! Bullfrog is a waterproof sunscreen, SPF 18, highly recommended by raft trip leaders, available at REI stores in the western U.S. In the tropics, you will tan through these sunscreens. It's important to put more on after swimming and every 3 to 4 hours even if you aren't swimming.

Insects, etc. Any tropical area has more insects than you usually see in temperate climates. A biology professor once told my class that the reptiles had their age, the mammals are having theirs now, but he felt that the next would belong to arthropods (insects and all others with jointed legs). If you travel in the tropics you may feel that the insects have always had the upper hand! In warm damp climates they flourish. If you see ants or an occasional cockroach in an otherwise clean establishment, it is not a sign of filth but only means no one has mopped there

95

in the past few minutes. Relax and enjoy the fantastic array of butterflies, moths, and caterpillars that brighten garden and forest here.

At low altitude, several types of gnats, sand-fleas, etc. may appear (or you'll find later that they bit without appearing) in the evening. Insect repellent, especially around your ankles, can save you some bites.

HOSPITALS,

SAN JOSE	Address	Telephone
Clinica Americana	Calle ctl./1, Ave. 14	22-10-10
Clinica Biblica	Calle ctl./1, Ave. 14	23-64-22
Cinica Catolica	Guadelupe	25-50-55
Clinica Santa Rita (Maternity)	Ave. 8, Calle 15/17	21-64-33
Calderon Guardia	Ave. 9, Calle 17	22-41-33
Children's Hospital	Paseo Colón, Calle 20	22-01-22
Hospital Mexico	Autopista General Cañas	32-61-22
San Juan de Dios (Free emergency service)	Paseo Colón, Calle 14	22-01-66
Red Cross (Ambulance)	21-58-18	

OTHER CITIES	Telephone	Red Cross (Ambulance)
Alajuela	41-50-11	41-29-39
Cartago	51-06-11	51-04-21
Heredia	37-10-91	37-11-15
Liberia	66-00-11	66-09-94
Limón	58-22-22	58-01-25
Puntarenas	63-00-33	61-01-84

Clinicas are private hospitals, available to foreigners at reasonable rates. Others are social security hospitals which provide emergency services to foreigners. All have laboratories, x-rays, and pharmacies.

Photography

Costa Rica is a great place for photography, whether you're a professional or just carry an Instamatic. The tropical flowers and blossoming trees, wildlife, and constantly changing scenery offer more choices than you'll be able to film in one trip.

Those who've traveled with a camera in the tropics before know what they want to do. For those who haven't, here are a few suggestions:

For any trip, take time to know your camera well before you leave home. If it's new or borrowed, load and shoot some film and get it back to study before you start this trip. Read the manual and practice. Bring all the film you think you'll need for the trip, plus a bit more. Bring extra batteries for your camera and flash. Radio and electronic stores at home receive many stock items packed with silica gel and may be able to give you some to protect gear and film from dampness. You can get lead-foil envelopes made for taking film through airport security— but then carry all your film in your carry-on bag and ask that it be hand-checked instead of x-rayed. Some professional photographers recommend that you simply put all film in a see-though plastic bag so inspectors can see it in the original containers quickly when they hand-check your bag.

You are allowed to bring 2 cameras and any reasonable amount of film into Costa Rica, but should get your equipment list with serial numbers reviewed by a Costa Rican consul at home if you want to bring more cameras. Film is very expensive, 2 or 3 times what you pay at home. If you have to buy extra film during the trip, get it from a busy photo store like the IFSA store on Ave. Central across from the Cultural Plaza, where

Birdwatchers try to get closer to a pair of turquoise-browed motmots.

97

they sell enough so any film they have is fresh.

Color film is very sensitive to heat. I leave any I won't need on a coastal trip back with my baggage in San Jose. Both color and black and white film soften in high humidity. They may jam the film winding mechanism of your camera or their sprocket holes may break so they won't wind at all. I keep the film in its original cans in a sealed bag with silica gel and dry the gel weekly in an oven. I bring the exposed film back from a trip of 3 months or less and have it processed at home.

Electronic cameras are delicate creatures in the humid, salty air on the coasts. A small amount of corrosion forming on any contacts can stop them for the trip. Keep your cameras as dry as possible and wipe them off before storing even for the night. After a multi-day field trip, I remove lenses from cameras and put all bodies, lenses, and my binoculars in a container with silica gel at least overnight. Mildew growing between lens components is impossible to remove.

If possible, bring at least 1 backup camera, preferably not a super miniature whose parts are tiny and extra fragile. If you should have to get a camera repaired, you will be lucky if parts are available. The IFSA store can send you to the repair place they use. Note that batteries are considered accessories and your camera may be returned without them if you don't make the person writing the receipt list them.

I use 2 Pentax ME bodies, one loaded with black and white and the other with color (Kodachrome 64, though I bring a few rolls of faster film for forest interiors). The lenses I switch as needed are a Macro-Zoom 70-210 mm, 50 mm, 28 mm, and 400 mm. The wide angle lens is good for buildings inside, narrow streets, and tall trees. It will show the rim and bottom of a volcano. Both cameras stopped on one trip, one repairable and the other not during the trip. I took a repairman's advice and bought a Pentax K-1000 body when I got back. It's an older, larger, heavier model that takes the same lenses and isn't as automated, but it's much more rugged with fewer electronics to corrode. Now I carry all 3 cameras on trips.

I use a flash often to fill in shadows or get more light in the forest. A tripod or monopod is useful. I use filters to protect the lenses as well as correct light—yellow or green for B-W film and skylight or ultraviolet for color. If you're using fast film, you'll want a neutral density filter to cut tropical midday sun.

If the sky is overcast, a camera with automatic exposure will pick up so much light from the sky that it underexposes everything else. If you set the meter for double the light, the picture subjects will come out. When the sky is blue and you don't have glare off the sea, the automatic camera is fairly accurate. In the forest, it's wise to use a separate light meter.

I carry my cameras securely zipped in my camera bag instead of hanging around my neck if I'll be using them. If not, I leave them back at the hotel desk. Anywhere, but especially on the streets of San Jose, Puntarenas, or Puerto Limón, I watch or have a companion watch the bag while I take pictures or load film.

Arts, Crafts, Souvenirs

Costa Rican craftsmen make beautiful pieces from metal, leather, ceramics and tropical hardwoods. Artists paint designs derived from the Moors who invaded Spain on oxcarts such as those that used to haul coffee to Puntarenas and still work on back roads. In modern times, they paint the designs on trays, wall plaques, and oxcarts ranging from toy size to barbecue stands. You can watch them do it at small factories in Sarchí, near San Jose. Many tours as well as the public buses go there. All wooden crafts are generally less expensive there than in San Jose, though you can find any crafts in San Jose gift shops. Plain wooden trays, lamps, candlesticks, etc. show off the grain of exotic tropical hardwoods.

Beautiful chairs, tables, beds, and other furniture are made from the same woods. You may want to see if the shop can ship something home for you. Do be sure the wood was well-dried before a large or valuable piece was made. Two artists whose furniture is well-designed and built are Barry Biesanz, 28-18-11, in Escazú and Jay Morrison, 28-66-97, in Santa Ana, both a few miles west of San Jose. You can call for appointments and directions to their shops.

Several shops, some of them artists' coops, have a good stock of crafts in San Jose:

Gift shop in Hotel Don Carlos, Calle 9, Ave. 7/9.
Apple store on Ave. Ctl, near Pizza Hut.
La Galeria, Calle 1, Ave. 1.
Artesania CANAPI, Calle 11, Ave. 1
Mercado Nacional de Artesania on Calle 11, Ave 2.

The northeastern San Jose suburb of Moravia, is best known for leather crafts including wallets, purses, briefcases, and belts. Leather is comparatively expensive, though you can find good values in the zippered handbags some Costa Ricans carry, even in San Jose. A bag big enough for anything I'd want to carry around all day, plus a camera, was less than $20. In the weeks before Christmas, vendors have stalls in downtown San Jose that are worth checking. I've seen fine buys in leather wallets and writing folders at the weekend market in front of the National Theater.

Many gift shops have gift packs of Costa Rican coffee and the liquor departments in supermarkets (supermercados) have bottles of Cafe Rica, a coffee liqueur like kahlua. Bags of roasted coffee beans are cheapest in supermarkets, $1 a pound or less. *Puro* on the label means that no fillers or sugar have been added in roasting. Vanilla beans and extract are better quality here than you may be able to find at home.

San Jose has many art galleries with original works and prints by Costa Rican artists. Exploring the galleries is fun and some of the work is very impressive.

The gift shop in Parque Bolivar, the national zoo, has wildlife and rainforest posters and T-shirts made from photos of some of the animals that help benefit the park system.

A Costa Rican I asked said one could bargain anywhere, even in department stores. That may be possible if one looks native and speaks excellent Spanish. You might try it in the central market stalls, and you definitely should bargain with cab drivers. In most stores, the prices are fixed.

The central markets with individual stalls selling anything from cheese to birdcages are an experience. The ones in San Jose and Alajuela are expecially interesting. One useful item

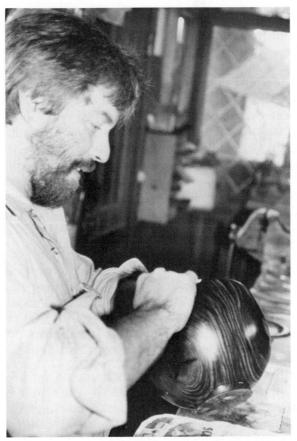

Barry Biesanz finishes a lignum vitae bowl in his wood arts studio in Escazu.

you'll find is the shopping bag made from rice sacks that the Costa Rican housewives use to carry purchases home. The bag is large, very strong, and is white or has the rice brand label and design on it. It costs less than a dollar and folds up to nothing in your purse, but is very handy in Costa Rica and back home for shopping and mail. The markets are the cheapest, most interesting place to buy a cotton canvas campesino's sun hat, cool protection, especially if you wet it before wearing. You've probably already gotten that absolute essential, an umbrella, but if you haven't, it's an excuse for some shopping. Downtown shops and the market stalls have folding ones made in Panama for $5 or less.

Returning Home—Customs

Most countries will not allow you to bring home birds, animals, or plants without a great deal of extra paperwork or permits. Some are prohibited outright, especially live endangered species or products from them. In Costa Rica, there are sometimes items made from alligators or jaguar or margay skins. These would be confiscated by customs at your port of entry if you should get that far with them. It's best to buy your orchid plants at home. If you've read this book, you probably have sense enough not to carry drugs across borders. Flights coming from Central or South American into almost any other country are particularly searched. A Labrador retriever worked the baggage carousel deligently in New Orleans when I returned from Costa Rica recently.

There's lots you can bring, much more than your airlines baggage allowance. You'll save time at the airport of entry by putting all your purchases and receipts for any expensive items together in one bag. Canadians absent from Canada for more than 7 days are allowed to bring in duty free $150 per year in value plus 40 ounces of liquor. Canada Customs publishes a useful brochure, "I Declare", that's worth studying.

United States citizens who've been abroad for 48 hours or more are allowed a value of $400 each, no matter what age. One quart of alcohol may be included if you're of age and the state you enter allows it. Useful pamphlets are "Your Trip Abroad" from the United States Dept. of State, Washington, D. C. 20520 and "GSP and the Traveler," from the Department of the Treasury, U.S. Customs Service, Washington, D.C. 20229. The latter explains the Generalized System of Preferences, which is a list of 2,500 products from developing countries, including Costa Rica, which are allowed into the United States duty free. Wood and metal furniture, but not wicker or straw, is one the list. So are some leather products.

While a U. S. passport isn't required for visits of 30 days or less to Costa Rica, it's a real convenience when you return to the U. S. Instead of having to prove your identity in a slow-moving line at the airport, you are almost waved through. Especially if you look awfully square and don't fit that fascinating stereotype the drug agents are looking for.

Living fence of poro trees grows from posts and now adds nitrogen to the soil.

LIVING IN COSTA RICA

Costa Rica encourages foreigners with a guaranteed pension income of at least $600 per month to become "pensionados", living in the country with all the privileges of a citizen except the right to vote and to work for hire (you can with a permit start a business which would hire locals). You are required to live in the country at least 4 months a year. Your passport must show entry and exit visas to document it. The intent of the law is to bring money into Costa Rica and to bring people with education and skills from whom Costa Ricans can learn. Thousands of people from many nations, including several thousand from North America, presently live in Costa Rica in any of several resident statuses.

Some are having a wonderful time, enjoying the friendly people, climate, low cost of living, and a new chapter in their lives. Others are like the retired aerospace engineer I met at the theater who has used his slightly impaired hearing as an excuse not to learn Spanish and who now spends his days in his apartotel watching TV. He hasn't thought to walk over to the university and volunteer to teach a physics or engineering

103

course in English to keep his brain cells alive. He's missing a lot of fun in becoming part of the country.

Edwin Salas was the inspired, imaginative head of the ICT's Pensionado Department. Officially, it's Departamento de Jubilados, Instituto Constarricense de Turismo, Apto. 777, San Jose, Costa Rica. Telephone, 23-17-33, Ext 264. His advice is the best I've heard: "When you're deciding to retire here, think about your attitude toward foreigners at home and then toward Costa Ricans. You'll find the villagers kind and generous as long as we don't feel rejected. Costa Ricans are very sensitive. An approved pensionado is a Costa Rican. Most U.S. citizens are scared by the language barrier. Don't be scared; it is not a barrier. There are so many fields in Costa Rica that the ground is fertile, but we need the seed."

There is a Newcomers' Seminar the second Tuesday of every month at the Irazú Hotel to which all are invited. More recently Newcomers' Seminars have been scheduled other Tuesdays at different hotels in San Jose. If you're thinking of retiring here, come and ask questions and meet others who already have. Some of the speakers at these meetings have investment projects to sell, but speakers do discuss any changes in the pensionado law, insurance for foreigners, and they answer any questions.

The **Asociación de Pensionados y Rentistas de Costa Rica,** Apdo. 6368, San Jose, Costa Rica (Phone 23-17-33, Ext. 264) is a good place to inquire for information even before you come to Costa Rica., if you're thinking of retiring here. They can send you a list of the requirements for pensionado status. Their office is next to the ICT Pensionado Office on the ground floor of the ICT building, av 4, c 5. Once you're in Costa Rica, they're good people to see for references to effective lawyers to get your residence status.

Costa Rica needs volunteers from babysitters to engineers and doctors. Sr. Salas took an inventory of much of the country's volunteer needs and would be very glad to point anyone interested toward a spot that could use his or her skills. It's the best way I've heard to get behind the doors and walls and meet interesting people as well as gain a sense of accomplishment. Volunteers have designed roads and helped train local medical helpers. The pensionado office has part-time volunteers who have designed its layout, put its records on computer, and who can translate many languages to help any retiree who needs it.

I think retiring here, or perhaps anywhere, is like the fenceposts you'll see along the road. If a dead log is set, it soon rots in the tropics. Costa Ricans plant live poro tree trunks with the bark left on. They grow into trees that work as fenceposts for a lifetime. You can keep living and growing, or rot.

If you're thinking of moving here, there are two pieces of advice you'll hear everywhere: come for extended visits in several seasons, including one of at least 6 months; and don't cut yourself off by handling your assets so that you can't return to your native country temporarily or permanently later if you change your mind. Since Costa Rican laws are different from the ones you have lived with, it's wise as soon as you have your residence status to arrange your affairs, including wills, with a Costa Rican lawyer so your personal and property rights are protected. Usually one member of a couple applies for residence, covering dependents. If assets can be divided to qualify both, it can save many problems in case of death or divorce. However then each would have to cash the required amount of money into colones annually.

The paperwork and procedure for becoming a pensionado are no one's joy. Start with ICT's advice in the Pensionado Office and talk to a lawyer recommended by other pensionados who've weathered the process. Be sure any time you deal with immigration that you have all the documentation of birth, bank and pension records they require, usually notarized by a Costa Rican consul near your former home and frequently translated into Spanish by an approved translator. Many people have done the whole procedure by themselves, and it is easier now that representatives from the other government departments are in the Pensionado Office, but most still recommend having a good lawyer do it.

You will be able to bring in any reasonable amount (including one of any usual household appliance and allowing 1 color TV and 1 black and white) of household goods once, and a vehicle every 5 years without paying the usual duties. For a vehicle up to $16,000 value including cost of transportation and insurance, you pay 15% tax on that amount. If the value exceeds $16,000, you pay the much higher Costa Rican duties on the excess. At the end of 5 years you can sell the car and import a new one on the same basis.

Do be prepared with patience to earn at least part of that pensionado status by outlasting the procedure for getting it. And then call the Pensionado Office and pitch in to make a contribution here!

Hired help for house and yard costs much less here than elsewhere, but you must get references from past employers for anyone who will be in the house when you aren't there. A good live-in maid is an excellent deterrent to theft, sometimes the only way you can be free to leave your house when you want to. Be prepared to explain exactly how you want anything done, if necessary in sign language at first while the maid teaches you Spanish! Many houses come with maid's quarters built in and you provide food. Costa Rican law provides for at least half a day off per week, holiday and vacation pay, and severance pay for anyone who has worked at least a year for you. With vacation and severance, you pay 14 months' pay for a 12 month year. You will also have to make social security contributions.

Your maid can help with or do the marketing and is a real asset when you bargain for produce or simply want to pay tico instead of gringo prices for anything not in major stores. She may be able to recommend seamstresses, haircutters, and neighborhood cab drivers who can be counted on at 5 a.m. when you need to catch an early flight. She can show you how to make tortillas, but you may have to show her how you want eggs fried.

Some neighborhoods contribute a monthly charge to have a night patrolman. In ours he pedalled around on a bicycle blowing a very loud whistle all night! This saved him the trouble of encountering a thief and woke most of us several times nightly so we knew he was on duty.

Costa Rican life runs at a more comfortable pace than in many other places, but you may have to get used to not worrying about whether something gets done this week or next. *Ahorita* means "a little now" literally, but really means (if you ask when the car will be fixed or when so-and-so will be back in his office) soon, sometime, next week, or maybe never! It's worse than *mañana*.

Papaya plantation.

If you want to bring a dog or cat into Costa Rica, you need to write ahead to Jefe del Departamento de Zoonosis, Ministerio de Salud, 1000 San Jose, Costa Rica, C.A. Ask for a form for Importation Permission. There will be a small fee required when you send it back (make a copy first in case it is lost in the mail). Allow time for the validated form to get back to you. You also need a health certificate signed by a local vet and certified by a Costa Rican consul. The health certificate needs to state that the animal is free of internal and external parasites, and in case of a dog, has had shots for distemper, hepatitis, leptosporosis, and parvovirus, and has a rabies shot at least 30 days old but not more than 3 years old. With all of this done in time, the entry is very smooth at the airport.

When I took my German Shepherd to Costa Rica for 2 months, I went first to her vet at home and got a store of worm pills and flea and tick dip. She caught a mild bout of canine turista probably from drinking ditch water on our morning jogs, but that easily cleared with terramyacin. Note that very shorthaired dogs are vulnerable to stinging insects and the screw worm fly which lays its eggs under the skin of livestock, leaving a large abcess with the larva. A medium coat seems to be adequate protection. I wouldn't consider taking any pet on a short trip as it vastly complicates finding housing—and, remember that $1 a pound in excess baggage!

Returning to the U.S. was simple. A Costa Rican vet filled out another health certificate which I took to the Dept. of Zoonosis in the Ministry of Health building behind San Juan de Dios Hospital, Calle 16, Ave. 6/8. It took just a few minutes and a few colones for the revenue stamp (much easier than getting my exit visa).You also need a Permiso de Exportación from Banco Central, which you can get as early as 15 days before you leave. All the U. S. authorities required at the border was the rabies certificate.

There are good vets and boarding kennels in the San Jose area. If you'll be living outside the Meseta Central, you may want to make up a pet medical kit. If you will be living on the coast, you might think again before bringing a cold weather breed. There are well-bred dogs available in Costa Rica.

If you're living any length of time and housekeeping in Costa Rica, you'll want *Living In Costa Rica,* published by the United States Government Women's Association, the embassy women's club. It lists suppliers of any repair or service you could need. The book is in all bookstores and gift shops.

Learning Spanish

You say you had 2 years of Spanish in high school 30 years ago, taught by the football coach because he had to have a few class hours? Costa Ricans appreciate any effort you make to speak their language. It shows that you care about them and their culture, besides making travel easier and allowing you to meet a wider variety of people than if you can only speak to those with English. They will help you with it and tell you words, unless they're too busy practicing their English on you. They also speak a bit more slowly than some Latin Americans which give you a chance.

If you can, take a class before you leave home. There are now some excellent taped language courses you can practice at home, from quick travelers' phrases needed in restaurants to the level the State Department employees are supposed to know. In between are some for the business traveler. Most of these now stress Latin American Spanish rather than 18th century Castillian. If you call the Spanish teachers at the nearest community college or adult education program, they may have a class, know where there's a Spanish conversation club, or help you find a good native speaker who'd like someone to practice English with in return. Classes in U.S. schools used to stress reading and didn't help you listen and speak very much.

In San Jose, there are excellent Spanish schools which teach short and long courses, some of which are very intensive. The **Costa Rican-North American Cultural Center** in Los Yoses has an excellent library and offers classes and programs at reasonable cost. It's a good place to meet people, both Costa Rican and foreign residents. In Los Yoses, on the main route leaving San Jose to the east. Apto. 1489, 1000 San Jose. Telephone 25-73-44. The Tico Times has ads for most schools, and we have a list in our Sources Of Information section at the back of this book.

You will be surprised how fast you can pick up some Spanish if you're not shy about trying to use it and make the effort to speak with local people instead of talking mostly to fellow foreigners. Spanish is probably the world's easiest language, and once you learn some, more doors are open in Costa Rica and you're set for travel all over Latin America.

House plants for export grow under plastic screen.

Investing in Costa Rica

We've mentioned agricultural projects for which you'll see investment advertising—for plantations of established and new crops such as macadamia nuts, jojoba oil, oranges, cardamon (spice), vanilla, and cashew nuts. You'll also see ads for real estate developments, either as raw land or condominimums, built or not yet constructed. There are industrial plants and tourist developments seeking investment capital.

You will have to make your own assesment of the projects and of the honesty and business sense of those promoting them. It's definitely "buyer beware." You're wise to live in Costa Rica for awhile, at least on extended visits, and see the project on the ground as well as look at similar projects before investing. You'll want to have someone honest with excellent Spanish, if yours is not, read any documents before you invest or sign. Many projects are promoted by foreigners rather than Costa Ricans.

Note also that many agricultural projects make heavy use of the pesticides and herbicides exported liberally by the U.S. chemical companies to developing countries where their use isn't banned or controlled as it may be at home. Sometimes the names of products are changed so you can't recognize tham (e.g. read the bill boards along the road up Irazú) and the instructions and cautions are written in English so the campesinos using them may not dilute or apply as directed.

Real estate in the Meseta Central is controlled as are building permits much as they are where you come from (check to see if you'll be able to build on the lot). Outside the area, some developers have simply run bulldozers wherever it would make the most lots without regard for the land, slope, or erosion. There are also some excellent projects (look during or just after the rainy season). When buying land, you must have a very careful lawyer. A friend attempting to buy acreage found there were two recorded deeds and that the land had two owners each of whom didn't know about the other!

Credit is expensive and often not available. Your real estate purchase will probably be on a cash basis—and so will the next buyer's if you later decide to sell. This is worth thinking about when you make the initial investment **and** when you add to its value with improvements. It accounts for many of the bargains you see in newspapers.

In addition to concern for the safety of your investment, it will be up to you and your conscience where you draw the line on chemical use, deforestation, or on real estate developments which raise the price of Costa Rican land beyond the ability of Costa Ricans to buy their own—or send it to the sea more rapidly than nature intended. Some projects are extremely well designed and well managed. The choice is yours.

Apples are a traditional Christmas luxury in Costa Rica, and not many will grow here, but a few farmers have planted orchards.

San Jose's government offices and banks give it a modern skyline.

REGIONS
Meseta Central

The Meseta Central, often called the Central Valley, is the heart of Costa Rica. High enough to be comfortable all year just north of the equator, with never a frost, and with little need for either heat or air conditioning, it's an ideal climate for people, most flowers and plants, and for doing whatever you want to almost any day of the year. Here there's a variety of scenery at every turn. Each village has a different character to explore, and the center of it all is bustling San Jose.

San Jose

San Jose is by far the largest city in the country, surrounded by a cluster of communities whose residents commute to work in the city daily. All national capitals should be this size—just big enough to be a city with fine restaurants, night clubs, excellent hotels in all price ranges, and cultural activities of all kinds. From discotheques, movie theaters with films in several languages, to big and little theater groups, sports events, art galleries, museums, shopping for anything, it's all here in a city small enough for you to walk around the central part in a day and to leave in a few minutes by bus or car. You can explore the city for a few days and vary your trip with day tours to nearby towns in the Meseta Central or up the nearby volcanoes as well as to each coast. People watching, night or day, is always entertaining.

When the stone sidewalks get hard, you can sit in one of the many parks for peace even a few feet from the busy streets. Do watch your step on the sidewalks as most are the responsibility for maintenance of the property owners they pass—and the stones and concrete vary accordingly. Some parks are the scene of weekly band concerts or art shows.

Stop by the ICT information desk under the Cultural Plaza at Ave. Central and Calle 5 for information and maps. Pick up the latest issue of the *Tico Times* at the newsstand on the west side of the Plaza, and you'll see what an array of choices you have. San Jose is really very easy to find your way around in, especially on foot when you don't have to worry about one-way streets. Do assume, however, that pedestrians have no rights, especially at corners where cars whip around from behind you. That assumption can save your life!

Costa Rica's Legislative Assembly building, a center of Latin American democracy.

San Jose's streets run north and south, the *calles*. *Avenidas* run east and west. Near the center of town is Avenida Central. North of it all the avenidas are numbered in odd numbers, to the south in even numbers. Actually Avenida 2 (Dos or Segunda) is a bigger boulevard in downtown than Central. On the west end of downtown, west of San Juan de Dios Hospital, Avenida Central is called Paseo Colón and is a wide, tree-lined street ending at Sabana Park. Calle Central runs north and south near the center of town and the streets to the east are numbered in odd numbers, to the west in even numbers. Numbers are usually on the corner buildings rather than on street signs. But there aren't any building numbers, and directions are in meters or varas from a corner. A block is supposed to be 100 varas long, a bit less than a hundred yards. An address might be given as "av 3 c 5/7". That means the building faces Avenida 3 on the block between Calles 5 and 7. It may be on either side of the street. It gets more sporting in the suburbs or out of town when everything is in meters from trees, bridges, or prominent buildings.

114

Tunnel under Cerro Zurquí on the new Guápiles Highway.

Besides the museums we've already discussed in San Jose, you might want to see the small national zoo (entrance on Calle 9, Ave. 11) where there are examples of Costa Rica's birds and animals. The zoo will be moved to a larger site in the western suburb of Santa Ana, but that isn't completed yet. If you're lucky, you might see one of the sloths in the trees landscaping the zoo. A small shop sells T-shirts and other souvenirs to help raise money for the zoo and other parts of the national park system. You can get information brochures about some of the other parks and their wildlife there as well.

The National Liquor Factory, a government enterprise, is on Calle 11 between Ave. 3/7. You can watch liquor made from Costa Rican fruits and sugar.

At night it's best to walk in groups if you go through the parks, but the Plaza de la Cultura is a busy spot and worth a stroll any night you're downtown. On a balmy evening, several small bands may be playing, teenagers dance to tape recorders, a student orchestra may be playing at the bottom of the stairs outside the ICT information office. street performers may be juggling—wander by and see what's happening tonight. You can often get tickets to National Theater performances even at the last minute, but it's best to get them earlier if possible.

San Jose is a city to enjoy, and the gateway to all the other things to see and do in Costa Rica.

Restaurants

San Jose has many restaurants to enjoy, from international restaurants like **The London Club** and **Lobster Inn** on Paseo Colón to simple tipico spots called sodas, and fast food chains including McDonald's, Mr. Pizza, and Pollos Fritos Kentucky. **Pops** has great ice cream, some flavors using tropical fruits like cas and mango.

The expensive restaurants advertise so heavily, particularly in tourist guide magazines and newspapers, that you can find them easily. There are some inexpensive to moderate ones that serve good food which you might have more trouble finding. Here are some my Costa Rican friends and I like.

Restaurant La Esmeralda, Ave. 2, Calle 5/7. Tel. 21-05-30.

Restaurante Los Antojitos, On Paseo Colón, Calles 26/28. Tel. 22-90-86. Also in Los Yoses in Centro Comercial Cocori.

Churreria Manolo, Ave. Ctl., Calle Ctl/2. Tel. 21-20-41.

Dennie's Restaurant, S.A., Ave. Ctl, Calle 19/21.

Restaurant Peppermint, Centro Comercial Cocori.

Restaurant Balcón de Europa, (Italian), Ave. Ctl., Calles 7/9.

Floridita, (Cuban), Ave. 1, Calle Ctl/2.

Escorial, Ave. 1, Calle 7/9, Tipico Costa Rican.

Manzana, Calle 11 or 13. Ave. Ctl. Tipico Costa Rican.

Tile-decorated shrine in San Jose park.

Where to Stay

San Jose hotels, more than others in Costa Rica, have a wide range of rooms in the same hotel. Most have junior suites and executive suites suitable for meetings. Our price ranges are based on singles before tax and service charges. Hotels are listed alphabetically within ranges, starting with luxurious.

San Jose hotels:

Aurola Holiday Inn: Convention facilities, separate exercise rooms for men and women, sauna, pool, casino. Wheelchair accessible. Live music. Most luxury in downtown area.

Cariari: Luxury hotel on grounds of Cariari Country Club. Attractive design, stonework. Presidential and bridal suites. Rate includes breakfast, full use of country club except golf green fees and horse rental. Tennis, riding school, jumping course, international class 18 hole golf course. Convention facilities, discotheque, casino.

San Jose (1)

	Aerola-Holiday Inn	Cariari	Sheraton Herradura	Corobici	Balmoral	Bougainvillea	Gran Hotel Costa Rica	Royal Dutch Suites
Price Range	A+	A+	A+	A	B	B	B	B
Cleanliness	exc	exc	exc	exc	exc	exc	V good	exc
Noise Level	exc	exc	exc	exc	exc	exc	mod	good
English Spoken	x	x	x	x	x	x	x	x
Pool	x	x	x	x		x		
On Waterfrnt								
Tv	x	x	x	x	x	x	x	x
Elevator	x	x	x	x	x	x	x	x
Bar	x	x	x	x	x	x	x	x
Restaur't	x	x	x	x	x	x	x	x
Parking	x	x	x	x	x	x		
Air Cond Or Fan	x	x	x	x	x	x	x	x
Courtesy Transp.		x	x	x	x			
In Town	x				x	x	x	x
W/Bath	all	all	All	all	all	all	all	all
Rooms No. Of	200	186	150	150	150	80	104	30
Telephone	33-72-33 US/1-800 Holiday	39-00-32 US/I-800 Cariari TELEX 7509 Cariari	39-00-33 US/I-800-3535 TELEX 75172 Herradura	32-81-22	22-50-22	33-66-22	21-40-00 TELEX 2131 HOTEL	22-14-14
Address	Ave 5, Calle 5Y Apdo 78702 1000 San Jose	Autopista Gen. Cañas Apdo. 737 Centro Colon San Jose, CR	Autopista General Cañas Apdo. 7-1880 1000 San Jose	Autopista General Cañas Apdo. 2443 1000 San Jose	Ave. Ctl. Calle 7/9 Apdo. 3344 1000 San Jose	In front of Edificio del Monte Apdo. 69 2120 San Jose	Ave ctl/2 Calle 5 Apdo. 527 1000 San Jose	Ave Ctl/2 Calle 4 Apdo. 4258 San Jose

Price ranges for single room: A+, over $70; A, $54-70; B, $36-54; C, $24-36; D, $14-24; E, $8-14; F, up to $8. Plus 13% tax.

Sheraton Herradura: Luxury hotel adjacent to Cariari. TV direct from U.S. by satellite. Church with mass in Spanish & English. Japanese restaurant. Health spa. Has golf package with 9 hole course at Los Reyes Country Club. Convention facilities for meetings of 10-200 people. Both hotels above are between airport and San Jose.

Corobicí: Near Sabana Park at west end of San Jose. Many rooms with view of mountains. Wheelchair accessible. Tennis, sauna, large pool in court with bandstand. Convention facilities. Casino.

Balmoral: Conversational lounges on each floor. Some interior rooms face center well. Double glass on street-facing rooms cuts noise. Rooms big. Convention facilities, casino, laundry, beauty shop, suites. Downtown.

Bougainvillea: Modern, very attractive hotel several blocks north of town center. Phone and wall safe in room. Wheelchair accessible. Tub and shower. Children's pool. Excellent food. Additional restaurants and nightlife in center nearby. Recommended.

Gran Hotel Costa Rica: Overlooks Plaza de la Cultura and plaza in front of National Theater. Inner court and garden with glass elevator. Casino. Dining room top floor. Coffee shop on ground floor with terrace is good place for sightseeing break. Will not keep baggage for you while you tour country.

Royal Dutch Suites: Family owned and operated. Big rooms with tubs and showers. Recommended.

Torremolinos: Cable TV (English), sitting area even in smallest rooms. Sauna, landscaped courtyard, quiet neighborhood at edge of downtown. Courtesy transportation to downtown. Conference room.

Ambassador: Outer rooms have mountain view over street, inner rooms face landscaped well. 6th floor all suites. Big rooms. Rate includes continental breakfast. Cable TV. Safety boxes for valuables. Allows pets on approval.

Fountain and Pre-Columbian sculpture in Hotel Don Carlos.

Costa Rica Tennis Club: On street off south side Sabana Park (with jogging paths). Rooms pleasant, on 2 floors. Some rooms with cooking facilities. Sauna, 8 tennis courts, bowling, basketball, huge pool often occupied by swimming classes. Excellent value.

Don Carlos: Delightful, quiet, small hotel in historic building with small courts, prehistoric sculptures. The only hotel in downtown San Jose that truly feels Costa Rican. Hospitable staff. Rate includes continental breakfast. Gift shop has well-chosen items at good prices. Recommended.

Europa: Some rooms with balcony overlooking pool in inner court, less street noise. Large rooms, suites. Some rooms wheelchair accessible. Excellent food.

Irazú: Biggest hotel in Costa Rica, just outside town on freeway. All rooms have balcony, tub & shower. Lighted tennis courts, beauty shop, sauna, casino, suites. Convention facilities. Exceptional value with these facilities. Some apartments with monthly rates. Has regular minibus to town. Taxis here extortional.

San Jose

San Jose (2)

Hotel	Address	Telephone	Rooms No. Of	W/Bath	In Town	Courtesy Transp.	Air Cond Or Fan	Parking	Restaur't	Bar	Elevator	Tv	On Waterfrnt	Pool	English Spoken	Noise Level	Cleanliness	Price Range
Torremolinos	Ave 5, Calle 40 Apdo. 2029 1000 San Jose	22-91-29 TELEX 2343 HOTOMOC	70	all	x	x		x	x	x		x		x	x	exc	exc	B
Ambassador	Paseo Colon Apdo 10186 1000 San Jose	21-81-55 TELEX 2315 Ambassador	71	all	x		x	x	x	x	x	x			x	exc	exc	C
Costa Rica Tennis Club	Sabana Sur Apdo. 4964 San Jose, CR	32-12-66	27	all	x		x	x	x	x	x	x		x	x	Very Good	exc	C
Don Carlos	Costado Calle 9 Ave 7/9 Apdo 1593 San Jose, CR	21-67-07	10	all	x			x	x		x				x	quiet	exc	C
Europa	Calle Central Ave 3/5 Apdo. 72 San Jose, CR	22-12-22 TELEX-3242 EUROPA	72	all	x		x		x	x	x	x		x	x	exc	exc	C
Irazú	Autopista Gen. Cañas Apdo. 962 San Jose , CR	32-48-11 TELEX-2307 IRAZU	350	all		x	x	x	x	x	x	x		x	x	exc	exc	C
Presidente	Ave. Ctl, Calle 7/9 Apdo. 2922 San Jose , CR	22-30-22	51	all	x		x	x	x	x	x	x			x	exc	exc	C
Royal Garden	Calle Ctl. Ave Ctl. Apdo. 3493 1000 San Jose	57-00-22	57	all	x	x	x	x	x	x	x	x			x	exc	exc	C
Alameda	Calle 12/14, Ave. Ctl. Apdo. 680 San Jose	21-30-45 23-60-83	52	all	x				x		x	x			x	good	exc	D

Price ranges for single room: A+, over $70; A, $54-70; B, $36-54; C, $24-36; D, $14-24; E, $8-14; F, up to $8. Plus 13% tax.

121

President: Deluxe hotel, newly refurnished, downtown. Phones. Suite. Inside rooms have windows to halls and skylighted wells, so are airy, quiet. Conference room. Ground floor bar and casino. Excellent restaurant. Our readers recommend.

Royal Gardens: Dining room well known for Chinese food, including breakfast. Pleasant rooms, well furnished, sitting areas. Suites. Quieter in back rooms. Casino.

Alameda: Rooms at back quieter. Light and airy. Cheerful dining room. Family style—no liquor or cigarettes sold, and no ladies of the street allowed. Phone in room. Up to 5 beds for family in some rooms. Neighborhood looks rough after dark.

Amstel: Well-run with super food. Rooms with air conditioning slightly higher. Rooms facing Calle 7 quietest. Central, good neighborhood. Excellent value. Recommended.

Fortuna: Family hotel. Beautiful Chinese restaurant with garden on ground floor. Neighborhood good. Weekly rates.

Galilea: Rooms quieter at back. Pleasant, friendly place. Student discounts. ½ block from Cartago bus station.

La Gran Via: Rooms at back very quiet. Front rooms have balcony overlooking street. Top floor rooms have great view and breeze. Two double beds all rooms. Cafeteria, coffee shop. Good value.

Park: Rooms open onto inner court. Weekly, monthly rates. Most residents North American men with escorts.

Plaza: Small lounge each floor. Faces central banking square downtown. Management helpful. Phone in room. Rooms small, but adequate. Good value.

Talamanca: Light, pleasant rooms, good beds. Rooms at back quieter, upper floors with view. Takes credit cards.

Costa Rica Inn: Manager very helpful. Tipico hotel in good neighborhood. Good place for budget traveler with limited Spanish to start in Costa Rica. (I did.) Usually has many North Americans who live in country. Weekly and monthly rates. Recommended.

San Jose (3)

Hotel	Price Range	Cleanliness	Noise Level	English Spoken	Pool	On Waterfrnt	Tv	Elevator	Bar	Restaur't	Parking	Air Cond Or Fan	Courtesy Transp.	In Town	W/Bath	Rooms No. Of	Telephone	Address
Amstel	D	exc	good	x			x	x	x	x		some		x	all	54	22-46-22	Calle 7, Ave 1/3, Apdo. 4192, San Jose, CR
Fortuna	D	exc	exc	x					x					x	all	29	23-53-44	Calle 2/4, Ave. 6, Apdo. 71570, San Jose, CR
Galilea	D	exc	fair	x										x	all	23	33-69-25	Ave Ctl, Calle 13, San Jose, CR
La Gran Via	D	exc	exc	x			x	x		x				x	all	32	22-77-37	Calle 1/3, Ave. Ctl. Apdo. 1433, San Jose, CR
Park	D	good	good	x					x	x				x	all	16	21-69-44	Calle 2/4, Ave. 4, Apdo. 4604, 1000 San Jose
Plaza	D	exc	good	x			x	x	x	x			x	x	all	40	22-55-33	Calle 2/4, Ave. Ctl. Apdo. 2019, San Jose, CR
Talamanca	D	exc	very good	x			x	x	x	x	x			x	all	50	33-50-33	Calle 8/10, Ave 2, Apdo. 449, 1000 San Jose
Costa Rica Inn	E	very clean	very good	x					x		x			x	all	35	22-52-03	Calle 9, Ave 1/3, Apdo. 10282, San Jose, CR

Price ranges for single room: A+, over $70; A, $54-70; B, $36-54; C, $24-36; D, $14-24; E, $8-14; F, up to $8. Plus 13% tax.

Diplomat: Pleasant, cheerful rooms, quieter at back. Good neighborhood.

Petit: Very pleasant with good beds. Manager helpful, friendly with no English, but guests usually do speak it. Most guests are returnees. Some rooms have sitting rooms. Cheerful, in fine neighborhood. Light cooking possible. Bi-weekly, monthly rates. Excellent value. Recommended.

Ritz: North American manager. Guests are foreign students, businessmen. Friendly place. Breakfast served. Rooms at back quieter, all somewhat dark. Lobby with TV, plants.

Troy's: Small friendly place with North American manager just east of central city. Simple meals served. Lobby with cable TV in English. Good value.

Asia: Helpful Chinese manager. Rooms quieter at back. Small lounge. Basic, but safe and clean. Good value.

Astoria: Basic but has hot water and washing machine. Most rooms don't have windows. Garden courtyard in back, TV in lobby.

Bella Vista: Some rooms have windows open to center, planted well—quiet. Not all rooms have windows. Hot water. Two floors.

Boston: Rooms larger than most similar hotels. Back rooms quieter, open to stairwell. Hot water. Good neighborhood.

Centroamericano: Room windows open to hall with plants. No street noise. Small lobby with TV. Hotel busy with foreign and tico residents. Friendly place, permissive with street friends.

Cororí: Back rooms quieter. Looked very good in 1983, but manager refused to show rooms in 1987. Clean soda downstairs. Rough neighborhood but Cocorí is best in it, adjacent to bus to Liberia.

Generaleño: Clean, friendly, basic. Rooms at front and back have windows, ones in between do not. Each floor has hall

San Jose (4)

Hotel	Address	Telephone	Rooms No. Of	W/Bath	In Town	Parking	Restaur't	Bar	Elevator	Tv	English Spoken	Noise Level	Cleanliness	Price Range
Diplomat	Calle 6, Ave Ct 1/2, Apdo. 6606, 1000 San Jose	21-81-33 21-87-44	30	all	x		x	x	x	x	x	very good	exc	E
Petit	Calle 24, Ave Ct/2, Calle 24, No. 39 S, San Jose, CR	33-07-66	14	7	x	x	x	x				exc	exc	E
Ritz	Calle Ctl, Ave 8/10, San Jose, CR	22-41-03	15	9	x		x				x	good	good	E
Hotel Troy	Ave 2, Calle 19/21, San Jose, Cr	22-67-56	5	2	x						x	high	very good	E.
Asia	Calle 11, Ave Ctl/1, San Jose, CR	23-38-93	19	5	x						x	high	very good	F
Astoria	Ave 7, Calle 7/9, San Jose, CR	21-21-74	18	2	x							high	very good	F
Hotel Bella Vista	Ave Ctl, Calle 19/21, Apdo. 3151, San Jose, CR	23-00-95	17	all	x		x	x			x	high	very good	F
Boston	Ave 8, Calle Ctl/2, San Jose, CR	21-05-63	23	16	x							good	good	F

Price ranges for single room: A+, over $70; A, $54-70; B, $36-54; C, $24-36; D, $14-24; E, $8-14; F, up to $8. Plus 13% tax.

balcony overlooking Ave. 2. Some rooms have shared baths. Doors have hasps on which one could provide own lock. Good value.

Johnson: Sitting area each floor. Hotel begins on second floor of building and has elevator from there. Phones. Restaurant serves breakfast only. Good value.

Musoc: Clean but basic. Hot water in shower only. Rough neighborhood overlooking Coca Cola bus terminal.

Pension Americana: Very clean though beds worn. Friendly, basic hotel in good neighborhood, doesn't allow guests in rooms. Dormitory and single rooms same price per person, about $3. Ask for rooms with windows. Lobby with TV. Family place used by ticos.

Pension Otoyo: Pleasant owner with limited English has been in business for 30 years. Light and airy with tile hallways, plants, TV in lobby. Tipico basic hotel in good neighborhood. Good value.

Pension Centro Continental: Basic hotel downstairs from Ritz. 4 rooms have windows, rest don't. Light lobby. Friendly. Some American guests.

Poás: Very basic, but clean, hotel with hot water in good neighborhood for about $4. All rooms share bath. Clean, inexpensive soda at front. Street level.

Toruma Youth Hostel.

San Jose (5)

Hotel	Address	Telephone	Rooms No. Of	W/Bath	In Town	Price Range	Cleanliness	Noise Level	English Spoken	Elevator	Bar	Restaur't
Centroamericano	Calle 6/8, Ave 2, Apdo. 3072, San Jose, CR	21-33-62	45	all	x	F	good	fair	x		x	x
Hotel Cocori	Calle 16, Ave 3, San Jose, CR	33-00-81	26	all	x	F	Not Inspected	Not Inspected				
Generaleno	Ave 2, Calle 8/10, San Jose, CR	33-78-77	47	8	x	F	exc	good				
Johnson	Calle 8, Ave Ctl 2, San Jose, CR	23-76-33	52	all	x	F	fair	good		x	x	x
Hotel Musoc	Calle Ctl, Ave 5/7, San Jose, CR	22-94-37	44	28	x	F	very good	high	x			x
Pension Americana	Calle 2, Ave. Ctl. Apdo. 4583, San Jose, CR	21-41-71	32	0	x	F	exc	good				
Pension Otoya	Calle Ctl, Ave 5/7, Apdo. 2662, San Jose, CR	21-39-25	13	1	x	F	very good	noisy				
Pension Centro Continental	Calle Ctl, Ave 8/10, San Jose, CR	33-17-31	11	shared	x	F	very good	good				x
Poás	Calle Ctl, Ave 5/7, San Jose, CR	21-78-02	18	0	x	F	very good	noisy				
Toruma Youth Hostel	Calle 29/33. Ave. Ctl. Apdo. 323-1002, San Jose	24-40-85	10	8	x	F	very good	high	x		x	x

Price ranges for single room: A+, over $70; A, $54-70; B, $36-54; C, $24-36; D, $14-24; E, $8-14; F, up to $8. Plus 13% tax.

Youth hostel:

Toruma Youth Hostel: Central America's only youth hostel is on the north side of Ave. Central in Los Yoses, San Jose's eastern suburb, across from Kentucky Fried Chicken. To a taxi or bus driver you ask for "Albergue Juvenil Toruma cerca de Pollos Fritos Kentucky". Friendly atmosphere in a plain facility, though the older building means high ceilings and a breeze. Dormitories for 6-20 people. Hot water. It's open 24 hours a day, and guests can stay as many days as they wish. Soda serves 3 meals a day but guests cannot do their own cooking. Sometimes has live bands and cultural events, mostly musical. Less than $3 even for non-members of hostel associations.

Apartotels are actually apartments catering to weekly or monthly tenants who want cooking facitilities, room for families, and possibly the swimming pools and other amenities that most apartments here do not have. They are completely furnished, including linen and dishes, so you don't have to set up housekeeping. Most, like hotels, have some suites or larger units. Generally they are less expensive than hotels with the same facilities, but more expensive than apartments catering to long-term tenants. They are often used by embassy personnel and business families newly moved to Costa Rica while they look for permanent housing.
Apartotels in and near San Jose:

Conquistador: 200 mts. north of Almacen Electra and bus stop, San Pedro bus. Large pool with jacuzzi jets, wading pool, walled garden. Most 2nd floor rooms have mountain view. Cheapest are studio apartments, others have separate living room, all are roomy. Tiled floor, 3 or 4-burner stove. Pets allowed, $4/day. Recommended.

Don Carlos: On side street 25 m south of Kentucky Fried Chicken on Ave. Ctl. in Los Yoses. Roomy, quiet, secure and well equipped for entertaining. Mountain views. Same ownership as Hotel Don Carlos. Recommended.

San Jose Apartotels

	El Conquistador	Don Carlos	Napoleon	Castilla	Lamm	Los Yoses	Ramgo	San Jose
Price Range	C	C	C	D	D	D	D	D
Cleanliness	exc	exc	exc	exc	exc	exc	exc	exc
Noise Level	exc	exc	exc	exc	good	fair	exc	good
English Spoken	x	x	x	x	x	x	x	x
Pool	x		x			x		
On Waterfrnt								
Tv	x		x	x	x	x	x	x
Elevator								
Bar								
Restaur't	x		x					
Parking	x		x	x	x	x	x	x
Air Cond Or Fan						some		
Courtesy Transp.								
In Town		x	x	x			x	x
W/Bath	all	all	all	all	all	all	all	all
Rooms No. Of	29	9	26	15	20	23	16	12
Telephone	25-30-22	21-67-07	23-32-52	22-21-13 21-20-80	21-49-20	25-00-33	32-38-23	22-04-55
Address	Los Yoses Apdo. 303 San Pedro Montes de Oca San Jose, CR	Los Yoses Apdo. 1593 San Jose, CR	Calle 40, Ave. 5 Apdo. 8-6340 San Jose, CR	Calle 24, Ave 2/4 Apdo. 4699 1000 San Jose	Calle 15, Ave. 1 Apdo. 2729 San Jose, CR	Carretera San Pedro Apdo. 1597 San Jose, CR	near Tennis Club Apdo. 1441 San Jose, CR	Calle 17/19, Ave 2 Apdo. 5834 San Jose, CR

Price ranges for single room: A+, over $70; A, $54-70; B, $36-54; C, $24-36; D, $14-24; E, $8-14; F, up to $8. Plus 13% tax.

Napoleon: Coffee shop. Residential neighborhood near Sabana Park (3-4 blocks). Balcony, TV, phone. Some floors carpet, some tile. Cheaper rooms without kitchen. Kitchen units have 2-burner stove, very small cooking area. Pets allowed.

Castilla: Excellent quiet neighborhood off Paseo Coln. 1 and 2 BR apartments with living and dining room, parquet floors, kitchen and laundry room, 4-burner stove. 20% monthly disc. One BR apartments open to well, quiet. Two BR apartments have balcony facing quiet street. Recommended.

Lamm: Near legislative assembly. Very helpful owner speaks fluent English. Separate bedroom, kitchen and living room. Some suites with maid's quarters. Daily linen change. Laundry and dry cleaning on premises. 24 hour porter and switchboard service. Can order refrigerator stocked before arrival. Weekly disc. No pets. Recommended.

Los Yoses: Some without kitchen facilities. Floor plans vary. Some have BR curtained from living room. 3-burner stove, TV. Safety boxes. Medium-sized pool.

Ramgo: On quiet street across from south side Sabana Park. Supermarket 1 block. Has lawn with courtyard. All apartments have 2 BR, roomy kitchen, laundry room, 4-burner stove, color TV. Small pet OK. Weekly and monthly rates. Embassy personnel use.

San Jose: 1 BR apartments have no table, only dining counter. 2 BR apts. have table. Parquet floors. Living room has day bed. Apts. smaller than some. Weekly, monthly rates.

The following hotels in San Jose were not inspected. Most are basic to budget hotels. If that's your interest, you may want to look at them. I'd start with the ones that have both calles and avenidas in odd numbers, for a better neighborhood.

d'galah: This is apparently considerably better than budget, near the gardens of the University of Costa Rica. Rooms, suites, kitchenettes. Restaurant. Apdo. 208-2350, San Jose. Phone 34-17-43 and 53-75-39.

Outlying Hotels

	Mirador Pico Blanco	Posada Pegasus	Alajuela	Motel Cypressal	El Portico	El Tirol
Price Range	D	E	F	C	D	D
Cleanliness	exc	good	good	very good	exc	exc
Noise Level	exc	exc	high	very good	exc	exc
English Spoken	x	x			x	x
Pool		x		x	x	
On Waterfrnt						
Tv					x	
Elevator						
Bar	x			x	x	x
Restaur't	x	x		x	x	x
Parking	x	x		x	x	x
Air Cond Or Fan						
Courtesy Transp.	x					
In Town			x			
W/Bath	all	4	all	?	all	all
Rooms No. Of	11	5	22	12	13	10
Telephone	28-19-08	28-41-96	41-12-41	37-44-66	37-60-22	38-07-07 38-08-09
Address	Pico Blanco Box 900 Escazú, CR	Calle de las Filtros Apdo. 370 Escazu, CR	25 S. Parque Central Apdo. 110 Alajuela, CR	5 km N. Birri Apdo. 7891 San Jose, CR	4 km de Birri Apdo. 289 Heredia, CR	San Rafael de Heredia Apdo. 7812 1000 San Jose

Price ranges for single room: A+, over $70; A, $54-70; B, $36-54; C, $24-36; D, $14-24; E, $8-14; F, up to $8. Plus 13% tax.

The Institute for National Security Building which houses the Jade Museum.

American, Ave 7, Calle 2/ctl.**Capital**, Calle 4, Ave. 3/5. 15 rooms, restaurant and lounge. Phone 21-84-97. **Central**, Calle 6, Ave 3. **Lido**, Ave 3, near Calle 14. **Lincoln**, Calle 6, Ave. 10/12. **Principe**, Ave. 6, Calle ctl./2. This neighborhood wouldn't be bad. Phone 22-79-83 Apdo. 4450, 1000 San Jose. 48 rooms. **Rialto**, Ave. 5, Calle 2. **Sheraton**, Ave. ctl., Calle 12/14, 56 rooms. **Tala Inn**, Calle 11, Ave 7/9.

Outlying hotels in the Meseta Central vary from basic hotels you'll find in any town in the country to small super-deluxe quiet places on hills overlooking the valley. These include some of the plushest hotels in Costa Rica. Above Escazú in the hills you'll find:

Mirador Pico Blanco: Tropical landscaping with fine view of San Jose 1000 ft below. Dining room has volcanic rock wall with cascading water and inpatiens blooming. Rooms cool and attractive with Costa Rican flavor. English owner. Recommended.

Posada Pegasus: Front deck with great view of mountains and San Jose. Jacuzzi. Library of mystical books. The Cross of Alajuelita on top of the mountain is a scenic hour and half hike above. Children and trained pets welcome.

The Popemobile, used by Pope John Paul II when he visited Costa Rica, now in the National Museum.

In Alajuela:

Alajuela Hotel: Exceptional value in tipico hotel 25 m south of the central park. The 4 apartments with living room, kitchen, and 4-burner stove often reserved by tourists who can afford to rent them even while touring the rest of the country. Clean, quiet, not plush, with outdoor laundry area and pleasant lobby. Foreign guests could help you with Spanish, but if you're on a budget and don't have to be in San Jose, this is recommended. It's a quick bus ride to the airport.

In the hills above Heredia:

Motel Cypressal: Closed when we tried to inspect.

El Pórtico: 8km. above Heredia on slopes of Barva. Rebuilt after fire, it has polished burnt brick original dining room floor (beautiful), heavy beams and hardwoods. Large rooms. Sauna and jacuzzi. Helpful management. "We have lots of tranquility." They have smashing views and lovely nearby walks on slopes of Barva Volcano. Residents are often other Central Americans on weekends when reservations are a must. Cater to seminars during week. Recommended.

El Tirol.

El Tirol: Chalets in Alpine style. Meeting facilities, playground, hiking, birding. Near Castillo Country Club. French chef. Recommended.

Note that in this volcanic belt every hotel in San Jose has withstood an earthquake of 7.1 on the Richter scale. Emergency lights in stairwells and corridors come on in the event of a power outage. During an earthquake guests are advised to brace themselves in an interior doorway or get under substantial furniture, but not to head for the street until the quake is over. Earthquakes are rare and major ones rarer still. I haven't been in one yet in Costa Rica. They happen more often in any coastal California location.

Since the Roman Catholic church is the principal denomination in any Latin country, the Metropolitan Cathedral (Calle ctl, Ave. 2) and other churches are beautiful expressions of faith, and saints' days are important events. Parades you'll see in San Jose consist mainly of school students, appropriately for this peaceful country. Because San Jose is so cosmopolitan, you will find churches or assemblies of most other denominations in or near the city. If you don't find information on services for yours in the *Tico Times* ask the ICT or call the *Tico Times* office (29-89-52, 22-00-40).

Banking is a government monopoly with regulations designed not only for safety, but to control the flow of foreign exchange in a country which badly needs it. The branch bank across from the Amstel Hotel on Ave. 1, Calle 7, is open Saturday mornings. While foreign banks can't offer a full range of domestic banking services here, one way for North Americans to have money sent to you in Costa Rica is to have it wired to the Costa Rican bank yours corresponds with.(learn which one before you leave home). Most major credit cards will allow you to charge for cash in a foreign country. The American Express office is at T.A.M. Travel, Calle 1, Ave. ctl/1.

OTEC, the student organization, runs budget tours for students and teachers within and outside Costa Rica. Students and teachers from abroad should bring identification as to their status (a letter from school administration on letterhead will do, or bring an international student card). OTEC's office is at Ave. 3, Calle 3/5. Mail: Apdo. 323, 1002 San Jose. Tel. 22-08-66. There is no age limit for full-time teachers or college staff. For students, the maximum age is 25.

View across the hills at Pico Blanco includes plane salvaged locally.

135

Any hotel can do laundry or arrange to have it done. Laundromats may not be self-service, but do offer same-day laundry. In San Jose there is one on Paseo Colón near Restaurante Bastille (west of downtown). Lavantia Doña Ana, open Monday through Saturday, is on the Autopista a Zapote, 125 mts. east of Plaza Gonzales, near the Ministry of Public Transport in the southeastern part of town. There's another in the Centro Commercial on the north side of the road to San Pedro, a suburban district east of Los Yoses. Take the San Pedro bus on Avenida 2 and ask the driver to let you off at the right place.

Buses Unless you ride taxis all the time, you'll soon learn the bus routes you need though the others may remain a mystery. Downtown the Sabana Cementario bus runs an elliptical route from Sabana South to town on Ave. Central and 2 and back out on Ave. 3. If you're coming into town from western suburbs, you can catch it at any of several stops near Sabana Park for the ride downtown. Going back out, you can get off near the Coca Cola station area and walk the block or two to that spot to catch your bus home. Try to avoid doing this at rush hour or in the dark, especially the first time. From Los Yoses or San Pedro, the San Pedro bus can drop you a block from the Atlantic Railway station where there are lots of cabs or it's an easy walk downtown. The Alajuela buses leave from the Coca Cola area every 10 minutes or so and stop at the airport. Some are minibuses for a slightly higher rate. ICT has a list of station addresses and they can answer questions.

For buses to Puntarenas, Limón, or Guanacaste, it's wise to get your ticket the day before, and get there at least 45 minutes early to be sure of a seat. From Limón back to San Jose, you should do the same. If you get on these at the terminal, you have a much better chance of having a seat than if you get on at one of the stops.

Alajuela
(pop. 43,000)

Alajuela is a delightful town about 20 km. northwest of San Jose, easily reached by bus, and only a few miles south of the airport. Its cathedral is beautiful with hardwoods inside and dark red shining corrugated metal covering its dome. In front is the central park with a bandstand and spreading mango trees. Another park honors Costa Rica's hero, Juan Santamaria, killed in the battle of Rivas. There's also a museum honoring him which often has current art exhibits. The central market is interesting and open even on Sundays when you might be in Alajuela to catch the special bus that departs from the south side of the church on an excursion up Poás Volcano at 8 a.m.

Nearby attractions include Campestre del Sol a former country club, with swimming pools, gym and dance hall, open Tuesday through Sunday, 8-4. Tel. 42-00-77. There are soccer games in the stadium almost every Sunday. Between Alajuela and Atenas, there's a bird zoo with a small admission fee. The bus to Atenas can drop you off there. The driver won't speak English, so you'll have to plan what you want to say in Spanish and watch for the sign on the right side of the road several miles out from Alajuela, across from a tropical plant farm, "vivero."

Bosque Encantado (Enchanted Woods) is an amusement park in La Garita, with animal sculptures, pool and lake. La Garita also has a hydroelectric dam and many nurseries with house plants. It's fun to walk through such places and take photos if you're traveling and can't take them home. If you buy property in Costa Rica, you'll enjoy low-cost, beautiful plants including orchids. At La Guacima, there are car and motorcycle races on the track every weekend.

As we went to press, the **Villa Comfort Geriatric Hotel,** opened in La Garita. It's a senior citizens' hotel featuring another aspect of the growing health tourism business in Costa Rica. It offers special diets and 24-hour available medical care, recreation facilities and landscaped grounds, but does not consider itself a nursing home. We did not inspect.

North from Alajuela on the old road, or you can go back out on the autopista to another turnoff, are Grecia, Sarchí, and Zarcero. Grecia is the center of pineapple growing and has an interesting church entirely covered in dark red painted metal. Sarchi, as I've discussed, has factories making painted oxcarts in traditional designs and painting the designs on other souvenirs. The furniture alone is worth the trip to see. Farther along, Zarcero is famous for boxwood hedges shaped into animals, dancers, and even a plane and a helicopter! There are tours to these towns or you could see them all in a day with a car. Some of the Poás tours stop in Sarchí.

South of the airport, opposite Alajuela, is the spring Ojo de Agua (Eye of Water), where over 6,000 gallons of water a minute rush out, supplying water to the city of Puntarenas, several other towns, and several big, clean swimming pools and an amusement area. It's such a popular outing spot, that I'd recommend going on weekdays unless your purpose is people watching. In that case, go on Sunday and watch Costa Rican families having fun at one of their favorite places. You can get there by bus or car from San Jose (ask ICT for the bus stop and schedule).

School children in Heredia.

Heredia
(pop. 30,000)

Heredia, like Alajuela, is a provincial capital and one of Costa Rica's oldest towns. It's the center of coffee growing and there are several beneficios nearby where coffee is dried and hulls removed before shipping. It has an old church, now a historic shrine, with bells brought from Cuzco, Peru, in Spanish colonial times. Several very old buildings, including a Spanish-style fort tower, line the central plaza. From Heredia, the road goes over the mountain saddle between the volcanoes, Barva and Poás, to the northern plain. A side road winds to a meeting with the road from Alajuela up Poás, providing an alternate way if you're driving a car and want to see more country. In season you can watch coffee picking; drive carefully to avoid the loaded coffee wagons going from finca to beneficio.

Cartago
(pop. 30,000)

Cartago, 14 miles east of San Jose, was the capital of Costa Rica during colonial times and later until 1823. At the base of Irazú, it has been shaken by eathquakes during every eruption so there are few old buildings. Several roads and the railroad meet here, making it the marketing and social center for a large area. Buses run between San Jose and Cartago every 20 minutes. Public buses run from Cartago up Irazú with stops at villages along the road twice a day. From here you can also take buses to Orosí and Paraiso.

The parish church in central Cartago, La Parroquia, was damaged by several earthquakes and not rebuilt after the one in 1910. Instead it has been converted into a delightful walled park with ponds, shrubs and benches. The street in front of it was restored in early style cobblestones.

The Basilica of Nuestra Señora de Los Angeles (the Patroness Saint of Costa Rica) is a magnificent Byzantine church on the east side of Cartago. Inside is the tiny image of the Black Virgin, and the walls are lined with cases of the gold and silver gifts by pilgrims in thanks for healing miracles attributed to her.

Inside the Basilica are thousands of silver figures given in thanks by those whose prayers have been answered by the Virgin of Los Angeles. Each represents the body part or whole she is credited with saving.

Many are in the shape of body parts healed—hands, arms, legs, etc. The church is built over the spring where the image of the Black Virgin was found. Behind it is a shrine where water from the spring flows and where people bring bottles and other containers to take some of the holy water. The saint's day is August 2, Cartago's biggest annual celebration.

Southeast of Cartago, on the road to Paraiso, are the Lankester Gardens, started by Dr. Charles Lankester as an orchid farm. The farm is now run by the University of Costa Rica biology department and is open to the public for a small fee which helps pay maintenance, from 8 a.m. to 3 p. m. daily. The Paraiso bus from Cartago can let you off there, or you can take a bus tour from San Jose. Orchids are in bloom all year there, but at their peak in March.

The altar to the Virgin of Los Angeles, patron saint of Costa Rica.

Turrialba
(pop. 24,000)

Dropping down into Turrialba on either train or bus, you're passing the lower edge of Costa Rica coffee growing. The town is in a scenic basin at the bottom of Turrialba Volcano. From Turrialba or Cartago one can get by bus to the village of Pacayas, from which horses or 4-wheel drives will reach the top. There is another steep, beautiful climb over a shoulder of Turrialba Volcano to drop down to the eastern lowland. From the top of that ridge you can see the Caribbean Sea.

Orosi Valley

The Orosi Valley is a beautiful area and a fine day trip from San Jose. There are two scenic overlooks built by ICT with fine views of the valley, picnic facilities, play areas for children, and, at the one overlooking Ujarrás, a restaurant. The Reventazón River winds down the valley, dammed at the lower end by Cach Dam with hydroelectric project and lake. The village of Orosi is nestled at the head of the valley and has the oldest active church in Costa Rica, built in 1743. It has a small museum. Its simplicity says much about the struggling colonial farmers almost forgotten by Spain but keeping their religion.

Orosi has hot springs and several "balnearios", public baths. The road circles the valley and crosses Cachí Dam. You can visit the power house.

Below the power house is the river gorge rafted recently by some river guides working in Costa Rica. They scouted it several days before their trip, but arrived to find the water much lower. By phone they located the manager who asked "How much water do you want?" and then released enough for their trip.

On the north side of the lake is another ICT facility with picnic ground, camping area, playing fields, swimming pool, restaurant, and boat launching ramp for fishing on the lake.

The ruins of Ujarrás church, built in 1693 and abandoned in 1833 when the village was flooded and moved to higher ground, are now a historic shrine. Watch plants now growing between the stones on the walls and try to imagine what this place meant to people so far from Spain.

Turrialba is a good excursion by bus or tour from San Jose to visit the Centro Agronomico Tropical de Investigacion y Enseñanza (CATIE). CATIE is a 2,500-acre agricultural research

Headquarters of CATIE, the agricultural research station.

station devoted to the needs of the small farmer. Governments of many countries including the United States, Canada, Britain and West Germany support research into high producing, disease-resistant strains of coffee, bananas, cacao. Aside from pollution, the small farmer can't afford agricultural chemicals. Other projects include improved strains of plantain, palms, and livestock bred to grow on coarse tropical grass with little or no grain supplement. A tissue culture lab grows thousands of genetic replicas of each desirable plant for virus-free shipment in small containers all over the tropical world. Agricultural school instructiors and researchers in tropical agriculture from many countries study here, living in quarters on the grounds. The world's largest collection of books and papers on tropical agriculture is here, and the card catalog is in English. The station also has a collection of hundreds of palms as well as many other forest species. It's a fascinating place which you can only begin to explore in a day.

If you live in Costa Rica, you may want to talk to them about nursery stock and seed which they sell at very reasonable prices. Dairy products from CATIE are sold in Turrialba, and it is the town's biggest employer.

143

To tour the station with an English-speaking guide, call 56-64-31 and arrange an appointment. The bus from San Jose will drop you in town (it leaves from the same station as the Cartago buses), and the locals can direct you to the bus that goes by CATIE or you can take a cab from Turrialba. Some tour agencies in San Jose run tours there, and any of them would be glad to set up special tours for interested small groups. At presstime, Arnold Erickson from the United States is head of the public relations office there and gives an inspiring tour. If somehow what is learned here can reach the small farmer, there seems more hope of feeding populations without losing or depleting the world's topsoil.

Route of The Saints

South of San Jose, in the mountains south of the Central Valley, is Costa Rica as she was. Tiny villages cling to the steep ridges (note the contour of their soccer fields!) or cluster in narrow canyon bottoms, while the slopes between are a patchwork of small coffee farms. The main road is paved but side roads aren't as they follow stream banks or head up a slope you'd hate to send a mule. Practically all the towns are named for saints, San Pablo, San Pedro, San Marcos, Santa Maria, etc. Up the back dirt roads that are perhaps better done on foot or with a rented horse, you may hear the quetzal or meet the farmer driving his cows to pasture.

For a day circle you can start around in either direction. If you aren't stopping overnight, you can avoid the afternoon fog on the Inter-American Hwy. crest by driving to Cartago in the morning and south on the highway to Empalme, where you turn right at the Texaco station and head down the Pacific slope. If you're traveling in the other direction, you take the road south from San Jose to Aserrí, and then to Tarbaca, Frailes, etc. This area is at 3-6000 ft altitude, so it's cool and comfortable.

I'd love to spend a few days or a quiet week in a town like Santa Maria de Dota, a delightful, clean village (easily reached by bus from San Jose) exploring the surrounding hills and valleys on foot and horse. These villages haven't been mobbed by tourists, and probably never will be. What a peaceful way to improve Spanish, meet people, and forget what hurrying is!

Hotel Dota in Santa Maria was temporarily closed for lack of business, but has a great collection of old tools and weapons on the walls downstairs, and would have opened for a phone call. (74-11-93, 9 rooms, about $3 single), half a block from the plaza. If I were staying longer, I'd rent a small house and settle in for a month. That has to be the best reason I've heard for not being glued to a computer for one's writing projects.

The East Coast

The railroad from San Jose to Puerto Limón opened the rest of the world to the Costa Ricans and their exports. Much more recently a winding road was added, not following the railroad, but connecting all the major towns along the way, Cartago, Turrialba, and Siquirres. By car, bus, or truck, this was much faster than the train but still took three and a half hours. Climbing and dropping down steep grades, it was hard for the heavily loaded trucks coming up from the port on the East Coast. The time and distance did limit weekend traffic to the beaches south of Limón.

In 1987 the long-awaited Guápiles Highway opened, shortening driving time from San Jose to two and a quarter hours by going under the Volcano Barva in a tunnel and down through Braulio Carrillo National Park (making it the most accessible in the country) to Guápiles and then to Limón.

Suddenly the coast has become an easy weekend trip, and it is crowded on weekends and holidays. If you drive, do not count on getting gas at Guápiles. In a few years the facilities will catch up with the crowds and the novelty will wear off. Meanwhile, enjoy the fast, scenic route, but be sure you have reservations if you're using hotels or cabinas. At presstime there was a toll for using the road, but you would save more than that in gas. You might want to go one way by the old road or the train just for variety in scenery. On the new road the distance from San Jose (go north on Calle 3) is about 165 kilometers, slightly over 100 miles.

145

Waterfront sculpture at Puerto Limon.

Puerto Limón
(pop. 39,000)

Puerto Limón, capital of the province of Limón, is the only port and the only town larger than a village on Costa Rica's East Coast. Throughout this book, we've used Puerto Limón and Limón interchangeably as the people do. After Columbus's landing here in 1502, a permanent Spanish settlement was still delayed for many years by raiding pirates and the lack of obvious wealth. Construction of the railroad to San Jose and the introduction of Jamaican blacks adapted to the climate led to its growth as Costa Rica's eastern port. Today it's a busy town with modern port facilities being built at Limn and at Moin, its northern suburb.

As it was in Columbus's time. Limón still is hot and humid, and is significant for the tourist mainly as the gateway to attractions north and south and as the end of train or bus from San Jose. The waterfront central park is a pleasant early morning or late afternoon walk with its ornate bandstand and the chance of seeing some of the resident sloths in its trees (look for a motionless blob that looks as if the tide washed it up there, especially on the south side of the park).

Normally sloths only climb down their trees every 7 or 8 days to defecate, but in the dry season these may come down more often for water from park fountains. Local people who find them in the street set them back on their trees, carefully avoiding their 3-inch claws. You may see them peering myopically above or eating a few leaves between naps. For aerobic exercise a sloth scratches his tummy.

There's a small library and roofed open study area for children amid the trees and flowers. Men and boys fish with throw lines from the stone seawall. Several blocks away the central mercado is interesting and has fresh fruit and other supplies you'll want if you're going to stay in villages like Cahuita and Puerto Viejo to the south or in the basic cabinas at Tortuguero.

Like San Jose, Puerto Limón has numbered calles (north-south) and avenidas (east-west, away from shore), except that there are no signs even on buildings and none of the residents seem to have heard of the system! As the shoreline curves deeply into downtown, it's hard to keep count even if you try. If you ask where a hotel is, people will tell you it's so many meters from the park, mercado, or a small radio station. You head in that direction and ask again, or take a cab. Fortunately, distances in the downtown area are short and many people are blacks who speak English. There are frequent public buses to Moin which go through Portete.

Columbus Day, October 12, is Limón's big annual festival with street dancing and parades, calypso and reggae music, and several days of celebrating. Hotel reservations then are a must, though if you can get them in hotels outside Limón, you'll probably get more sleep.

Most North Americans staying in Limón will require at least a fan keeping air moving to be able to sleep. There are budget and basic hotels in Limón, reviewed below. However, if you can afford more and don't have to catch a 5:30 a.m. bus, it's worth going to one of those at Portete, several miles north. At Moin, the ICT built a facility including swimming pool, picnic and camping area. Playa Bonita at Portete is Limón's swimming beach.

147

Where to Stay

Puerto Limón:

Acón: Dining room and food are good. Hotel is the best in town, but noisy on weekends when discotheque on second floor swings. All others downtown are quite basic.

Miami: Rooms at back quieter. Soda restaurant serves tipico and Chinese food. Ask for demonstration of air conditioning or fan and hot water on shower head.

Gran Hotel Los Angeles: Across from mercado. Rooms with air conditioning slightly higher price. Hot water. Refused to show rooms.

International: On quiet street. Cold water only. Refused to show rooms. Chinese restaurant.

Lincoln: Next door to Internacional on same quiet street. Some rooms have no windows and only 5 have air conditioning (the rest have fans), but a good value in a very basic hotel. Pleasant manager.

Ng: Clean, basic. OK.

Park: Rooms facing sea have fresh air, view and quiet. They fill early in day. Rooms facing street are on block with traffic, 2 cantinas and a firehouse, and without air conditioning, you'll want to open window. Rooms dirty. Dining room recommended. Located 2 blocks from park.

Tete: Rooms at back quieter. New bathrooms. Across from mercado. Hotel is on second floor ringed by marble titled balcony with plants & seats. Helpful manager speaks English.

Not inspected: **Caribe**, 58-01-38, 13 rooms. Having found clean if basic rooms for as little as 80 colones near the market and in the next few blocks north, I avoided the rough neighborhood with basic hotels and cantinas near the railroad station.

	Acón	Miami	Gran Hotel Los Angeles	Internacional	Lincoln	Ng	Park	Tete
Price Range	D	E	F	F	F	F	F	F
Cleanliness	good	good	good	very good	very good	good	exc	exc
Noise Level	high	fair	fair	exc	exc	high	high	high
English Spoken		x						
Pool								
On Waterfrnt							x	
Tv								
Elevator								
Bar	x		x				x	
Restaur't	x		x				x	
Parking		x						
Air Cond Or Fan	x	x	x	x	x	x	x	x
Courtesy Transp.								
In Town	x	x	x	x	x	x	x	x
W/Bath	all	all	all	all	all	all	all	all
Rooms No. Of	37	30	28	20	14	11	25	14
Telephone	58-10-10	58-04-90 58-10-88	58-20-68x	58-04-34	58-00-74	58-21-34	58-34-76	58-00-51 58-11-22
Address	Calle 3, Ave 2 Apdo. 528 Puerto Limón, CR	Calle 4/5 Ave 2 Apdo. 266 Puerto Limón, CR	Across from Mercado Apdo. 514 Puerto Limón, CR	Ave 5, Calle 2/3 Apdo. 288 Limón, CR	Ave 5, Calle 2/3 Apdo. 888 Limón, CR	Ave 5, Calle 3 Apdo. 145 Limón, CR	Ave 3, Calle 1/2 Apdo. 35 Puerto Limón, CR	Central Ave Apdo. 401 Puerto Limón, CR

Puerto Limón

Price ranges for single room: A+, over $70; A, $54-70; B, $36-54; C, $24-36; D, $14-24; E, $8-14; F, up to $8. Plus 13% tax.

Portete:

Matama: Deluxe, comfortable concrete cabinas for 6 on land-scaped grounds across highway from sea. (2 BR plus loft each) Attractive dining room and lounge. Aviary and tapir on grounds.

Cabinas Cocori y Marbella: Fairly basic cabinas for 4 on water-front across from Metama, beside small rocky cove, with swimming. Linen not provided.

Las Olas: Deluxe hotel built over beach rocks with covered open air dining overlooking surf and swimming pool. Wheelchair ramp from parking area, sauna (in Limón!), casino. Corner suites with sea view in 2 directions, balcony and sitting room. Excellent value. Organized tours to Cahuita, Tortuguero and Isla Uvita. I have stayed here and liked it. However, more recently the manager refused to let us see rooms. Said price would be raised shortly, so it may be higher than we show.

Puerto Limón has no bus station, but there are several main bus stops with ticket windows for buses to San Jose and south through Cahuita and Puerto Viejo to Bribri and Sixaola on the Panamanian border, "la frontera." You should buy bus tickets the day before to be sure of getting on and then get there early to get a seat.

SANSA has daily flights between Limón and San Jose, landing at the airport along the road south of town. There's an office downtown in Limón as well as in San Jose.

Taxis wait along the west side of the mercado, even at 5 a.m. when you want to go to Moin to catch a boat. Sometimes you can arrange a reasonable price for a day tour or drop-off at Cahuita or Puerto Viejo for a small group at the time you want to go .

South of Limón there are beaches all along the coast, some with excellent swimming like Cahuita and Puerto Viejo. To the north there are sharks and muddy water from the rivers emptying into the sea. While some people swim at Tortuguero, it can be risky. The sharks follow channels back into fresh water

Portete

	Matama	Cabinas Cocori Y Marbella	Las Olas
Price Range	C	E	D
Cleanliness	good	good	good
Noise Level	exc	exc	exc
English Spoken	x		x
Pool	x		x
On Waterfrnt		x	x
Tv			
Elevator			
Bar	x		x
Restaur't	x		x
Parking	x		x
Air Cond Or Fan	x	x	x
Courtesy Transp.			
In Town			
W/Bath	all	all	all
Rooms No. Of	8	4	49
Telephone	58-11-23	58-29-30	58-14-14
Address	Playa Bonita on road to Portete Apdo. 686 Puerto Limón, CR	Portete	Carretera Portete Apdo. 701 Puerto Limón, CR

Price ranges for single room: A+, over $70; A, $54-70; B, $36-54; C, $24-36; D, $14-24; E, $8-14; F, up to $8. Plus 13% tax.

Cacao, source of chocolate.

and some go all the way up the San Juan River to Lake Nicaragua. Scientists only recently learned that these sharks move freely back and forth between fresh and salt water.

North From Puerto Limón

Having already described the canales as an unforgettable experience for any nature-lover, I won't go into detail here.

Presently accomodations range from basic cabinas to deluxe fishing lodges, with nothing in between. Most fishermen using the lodges book weekly package plans before leaving the U.S. or Europe and then fly into the lodge by air taxi. For the very low budget traveler with more time, one could use basic rooms at Tortuguero or Barra Colorado and hire a villager with skiff. Wildlife viewing would then depend on the knowledge of the person you picked.

At Moin, ICT developed a recreation area with pool, camping, and boat dock for La Samay, the government boat which runs to Barra once a week on Thursdays, and to Tortuguero on Saturdays, returning Sunday. The Rio Colorado Lodge and Isla de

Pesca run tours the full length of the main canal from Moin to Barra and their lodges there. Costa Rica Expeditions runs special nature tours up the quiet back channels from Tortuguero with biologists. Shy species such as the manatee are more likely there. Nature tours generally have to be booked well ahead. Other tour agents are planning tours in the area.

Where To Stay (south to north):

Parismina Tarpon Lodge: Open Jan-June for tarpon, Aug-Oct. for snook. Fly into local strip, or ride boat short distance from Moin. Rate includes meals, boat, motor and fishing guide.

Tortuga Lodge: Deluxe lodge across channel from village, serves fishermen and nature tours. Open all year. Fishing is for tarpon, shark and bass in spring; snook, shark, and bass in fall. Green turtles lay eggs on the beach in summer and early fall with hatching 2 months later, running into November.

Tortuga Lodge.

Northeastern Region

	Parismina Tarpon Ranch	Tortuga Lodge	Sabina's Cabinas	Rio Colorado Lodge	Isla de Pesca	Casa Mar
Price Range	A+	B	E	B	A	A
Cleanliness	exc	exc	exc	exc	exc	exc
Noise Level	exc	exc	exc	exc	exc	exc
English Spoken	x	x		x	x	x
Pool						
On Waterfrnt	x	x	x	x	x	x
Tv						
Elevator						
Bar		x		x		x
Restaur't	x	x		x	x	x
Parking						
Air Cond Or Fan	x	x		x	x	
Courtesy Transp.					x	
In Town			x			
W/Bath	all	all		all	all	all
Rooms No. Of	13	18	31	12	12	12
Telephone	35-77-66	S.J. 23-03-33 Lodge 71-68-61	71-80-99	32-40-63 32-86-10	32-82-19 32-22-79	41-28-20
Address	Parismina Apdo. 149 Moravia, CR	Tortuguero Apdo. 6941 San Jose, CR	Barra del Tortuguero	Barra del Colorado Apdo. 5094 San Jose, CR	Barra del Colorado Mel Schneider 150 E Ontario St. Chicago, IL 60611	Barra del Colorado Apdo. 825 Centro Colón San Jose, CR

Price ranges for single room: A+, over $70; A, $54-70; B, $36-54; C, $24-36; D, $14-24; E, $8-14; F, up to $8. Plus 13% tax.

Downtown Tortuguero.

Dugout canoe almost finished in Tortuguero.

Sabina's Cabinas: In village of Tortuguero near boat landing. Basic rooms upstairs slightly higher, but have smashing view of beach and catch breeze. There are other basic rooms not inspected, also in village. Small restaurant and pulperia. All adjacent to beach.

Rio Colorado Lodge: open all year for tours as well as fishing. Can add days to 2 day tours or join tour in Limón if you want to ride train from San Jose. Excellent food, friendly place and staff. Office in Corobic Hotel, San Jose.

Snook is good eating, and the cats know it too!

Cabins at Isla de Pesca.

Isla de Pesca: Deluxe fishing lodge open mid-Jan-May 31; Aug.-Oct. 31. Duplex cabins. Tackle shop with sales, rentals. Rates negotiable if group can be coordinated with flight required by another group going or coming. Recently has added tours up canales with their own boat.

Casa Mar: Deluxe (most on coast) fishing lodge, open Jan. to June for tarpon and late Aug. to Nov. for snook. Package fishing trips include almost everything. Duplex cabins, excellent food. Many repeat fishermen.

Rates at all lodges include meals. Fishing tours include boats, guides, equipment, and flight to camp as indicated in package. Some serve liquor extra and some it's bring your own. Guides are tipped and hotel staff is too if a service charge isn't added.

Charter plane from San Jose picks up passengers at Barra Colorado.

Barra Colorado is divided by the Rio Colorado with separate villages, Barra Nord and Barra Sud. The airstrip and a basic hotel, not inspected, are at Barra Sud. At Barra Nord there are basic cabinas, also not inspected. High tides and rains can leave both villages soggy and they aren't well lit at night. If you're using basic accommodations, try to avoid a night arrival. The beach at Barra Sud is a steep, wild place not for swimming, but an inspiring walk with driftwood and surf. Sunsets here are some of the world's finest.

South From Puerto Limón

The coastal villages of Cahuita and Puerto Viejo are relaxed places in the Caribbean style of 50 years ago, except for the juke boxes in the cantinas. Accommodations range from budget to basic though clean. Hint—do bring toilet paper as many of the basic places don't furnish it. Note also that fruit isn't generally available in town, and you may want to bring hiking food with you. Local stores sometimes sell bread made with coconut by the local women. You'll meet their children on the street with baskets of it, still hot. You can relax, swim, walk roads and paths to see birds, flowers, monkeys and butterflies, and meet nice people (some of whom are quoted in Paula Palmer's book, *What Happen*). Absorbing the feeling of these villages and understanding what it's like to live here takes time. After 4 days in Cahuita, I began to feel in pace and not to feel a reason to hurry, or any "must-dos."

The new highway from San Jose to Puerto Limón and the paved road to Cahuita are changing the tempo of life here, especially on holidays and weekends when you may prefer to be somewhere else. Until there are better hotels built in the area, accommodations are fairly basic and the noise level "downtown" in Cahuita can be bad. Come mid-week and enjoy it.

Living is cheap—you'll have to drink a lot to spend more than $25 a day, and you can get by on less. However the pressure of increased tourism due to roads that had just opened when we inspected, could lead to price increases later. You may find them higher than we quote here. If you want deluxe hotel rooms, you could stay at Portete and make a day trip south.

Cahuita is larger and more urban, if you can say that about either, than Puerto Viejo. The national park with coral reef adjoins it on the south. Nearby are the hotel and cantinas, and a pulpera, small store with a few groceries and occasional fresh bread. Most of the cabinas are at the end of the point Cahuita is built on and down main street, left at the town power house and another quarter mile on toward the black sand beach. Either area is quiet, lit by fireflies at night.

Puerto Viejo's pace is even slower and more relaxed. It's built around a small bay with calm water for swimming right in front of town. Stanford's, an open-air restaurant overlooking the bay, is well-known for its seafood. In both villages, you'll find helpful, genial blacks who speak English, Peace Corps volunteers promoting cooperatives and fish farming, and young, former U.S. residents taking a temporary or permanent break from the hurry back home.

Where To Stay

Cahuita: (ranged as usual in descending order of price ranges as we found them, and alphabetically within the range, not by area of town).

Club Campestre: large pool, restaurant, bar. 15 rooms. Fans, but electricity is by generator which is off most of night. Caters to family groups. Range D.

Atlantida: 2 cabinas with fan, twin beds, on lawn adjacent to soccer field. Canadian owned, but owner not around when we inspected this time.

Hotel Cahuita: Rooms above and behind small dining room with TV. Food good. Cabinas in backyard probably quieter, and defnitely in better shape than rooms above hotel. However new owner, French-Canadian, has plans for overhaul and expansion.

Surfside Cabinas: Modern building on   Cahuita Point divided into 2 cabinas for 2-4 people. You can ask for fans. Excellent value. Mr. and Mrs. David Buchanan are pleasant, interesting mainstays of village. Recommended.

Vaz Cabinas: Modern concrete cabinas, across from Cahuita Hotel. Owner in Saloon Vaz. No screens. Need fans.

Black Beach Cabinas: Readers have reported well on A-frame

Cabinas Jenny: Basic rooms on Cahuita Point, outdoor cooking area. Canadian owned. Friendly, young communal atmosphere.

Grant's Cabinas: Separate rooms in cabins, shared bath. One cabina for 2 with shower. Across road from black sand beach. Owner Letty Grant delightful and helpful.

Palmer Cabinas: Large cabinas that can sleep up to 4. Fenced backyard. Sell much-needed items such as sunscreen, etc. Manager helpful. ½ block from town center.

Cahuita

	Hotel Club Cam	El Atlantida	Hotel Cahuita	Surfside Cabinas	Vaz Cabinas	Black Beach Cabinas	Cabinas Jenny	Grant's Cabinas	Palmer Cabinas
Price Range	D	E	E	E	E	E	F	F	F
Cleanliness	Not Inspected	exc	good	very good	good	fair	exc	good	good
Noise Level		exc	exc	exc	exc	very good	exc	exc	good
English Spoken			x	x		x	x		x
Pool	x		x						
On Waterfrnt				x			x		
Tv									
Elevator									
Bar	x				x	x			
Restaur't	x				x				
Parking		x	x				x	x	
Air Cond Or Fan		x	x	x	x	x			
Courtesy Transp.									
In Town		x	x	x	x	x	x	x	x
W/Bath	9	all	10	all	all	2	all	all	all
Rooms No. Of	9	2	15	4	10	2	7	5	5
Telephone	58-28-61	None	58-15-15 Ext. 201	58-15-15 Ext. 202	58-15-15 Ext. 218	58-15-15	58-15-15 Ext. 256	58-15-15 Ext. 206	58-15-15 Ext. 243
Address	Cahuita 1150 La Uruca Apdo. 214 Estero Negro Carr, Cahuita	Cahuita, Limón	Cahuita Apdo. 121	Cahuita Apdo. 360 Cahuita, Limón	Cahuita, Limón	Cahuita, Limón	Cahuita Point Apdo. 783 Cahuita, Limón	Cahuita, Limón Apdo. 64 Puerto Limón	Cahuita Apdo. 865 Limón

Price ranges for single room: A+, over $70; A, $54-70; B, $36-54; C, $24-36; D, $14-24; E, $8-14; F, up to $8. Plus 13% tax.

Hauling propane cylinders home in Cahuita.

Camping is possible at several sites among the palms and the trail south from Cahuita and there is a campground 3 miles south of Cahuita at Puerto Vargas, the park headquarters. You can hike there from Cahuita, but most people follow the main road south of town and turn in at the park entrance. It's less than half a mile to the campground from there—shaded, with trees for hanging a hammock. Bring everying you'll need except water.

Puerto Viejo:

Has public phone which may take messages. Unless equipped for camping, be sure you have reservations, especially on weekends. Several of the owners listed below are improving their rooms and building new ones, since the highway is bringing more travelers to the southeast coast. Shortly you should have alternatives to basic here. Stanford's is famous for seafood dinners and Bambu's has good food and prices.

Apartamentos Antigua Bohio: The only modern, better than basic rooms in town. Pleasant, large rooms, good beds. Rates for 4 and 8 nights.

Cabinas Manuel Leon: Basic rooms in long building. End units have windows on 2 sides, ones in between don't. Rates per unit for 1-3.

Maiti: Rooms basic, but screened. Downstairs cheapest, but upstairs light, airy. Manager helpful.

Maritza: Basic rooms on second floor which manager refused to show. 5 rooms in annex were inspected and found basic but clean and airy. Music in cantina below supplosed to be off at 9 p.m.

Several hundred yards north up the beach from the beginning of the village is **Cabinas Chimirui** with simple thatched huts near the beach. We didn't inspect, but readers report enjoying it and the Talamancan Indian owner who sells crafts and leads horseback rides in nearby backcountry.

West and Southwest
Puntarenas
(pop. 34,700)

Like Limón on the Caribbean coast, Puntarenas is a major port and perhaps more important to the tourist as a gateway to the Gulf of Nicoya and the Nicoya Peninsula than as a long-term destination. Buses and the electric train from San Jose can get you there in a few hours. Puntarenas fills a long narrow sandspit out into the gulf, only a block or two wide at the narrowest. To the south is the open end of the gulf with mild surf hitting the beach. To the north is a lagoon with mangrove swamps, very important to wildlife and fisheries.

If you look quickly as you pass mangroves (one of few trees that grow with roots in salt water) on the right as you start out on the spit, you'll see storks, roseate spoonbills, and other waterfowl feeding in shallow water a few feet from the busy highway. If you're driving, this is a good spot to stop for bird photography, especially early in the morning. Farther along in the lagoon is Costa Rica's Yacht Club and marina followed by the commercial fishing fleet and the ferry dock. Shrimp fishing

Hotel	Address	Telephone	Rooms No. Of	W/Bath	Price Range	Cleanliness	Noise Level	English Spoken	Pool	On Waterfrnt	Tv	Elevator	Bar	Restaur't	Parking	Air Cond Or Fan	Courtesy Transp.	In Town
Puerto Viejo Apartamentos Angiqua Bohio	Puerto Viejo Limón	58-08-54	2	all	E	?	exc				not inspected		x	x	x			x
Cabinas Manuel Leon	Puerto Viejo Limón	58-08-54	5	all	F	poor	exc	x		x				x	x			x
Maiti	Puerto Viejo Limón	58-08-54	18			good	fair											
Costa Rica Yacht Club	Cocal, Puntarenas Apdo. 2530 San Jose 1000	61-07-84	28	all	A	good	good	x	x	x			x	x	x	x		x
Los Chalets	Chacarita 1500 m Oeste Apdo. 1287, Punt.	63-01-50	18	all	B	very good	exc		x	x						x		x
Colonial	Cocal, Puntarenas Apdo. 368, Punt.	61-18-33	56	all	C	exc	exc	x	x	x			x	x	x	x		x
Porto Bello	Cocal, Puntarenas Apdo. 109, Punt.	61-13-22 61-21-22	34	all	C	exc	exc	x		x			x	x	x	x		x
El Joron	Paseo de los Turistas, Punt.	61-04-67	5	all	C	exc	very good	x		x			x	x	x	x		x
Las Brisas	Paseo de los Turistas Apdo. 83, Punt.	61-21-20	9	all	D	exc	exc	x		x			x	x	x	x		x
Tioga	Paseo de los Turistas Apdo. 96, Punt.	61-02-71	46	all	D	exc	exc		x	x			x	x	x	x		x
Los Hamacas	Paseo de las Turistas, Punt.	61-03-98	23	all	D	good	high		x	x			x	x		x		x
Castañuelas	Esparza	63-51-05	14	all	E	very good	very good								x	x		

Price ranges for single room: A+, over $70; A, $54-70; B, $36-54; C, $24-36; D, $14-24; E, $8-14; F, up to $8. Plus 13% tax.

is very important here and you may wonder why shrimp is the most expensive item on most menus. Most shrimp are exported and command a high price on the international market.

The railroad station at Puntarenas.

The *Calypso*, a yacht used for very popular day tours with gourmet lunch on a secluded island beach in the Gulf of Nicoya, leaves from the yacht harbor. They run a minibus down from San Jose and can pick you up at your hotel, returning you that night. There is a small boat charter service, Taximar, based at the yacht harbor, which takes individuals or groups fishing or cuising among the islands in the Gulf, about $35 for a boat holding 4-6 people.

The launch to Paquera on the Nicoya Peninsula departs from just behind the market at 6 a.m. and 3 p.m. Mon. thorugh Sat. This boat doesn't carry cars, but the bus to Cóbano meets it, stopping at Playa Tambor. The car ferry leaves at 7:30 a.m. and 4 p.m. Mon. through Fri. and 7:30 p.m., 11 a.m., and 4 p.m. Sat. and Sun. for Naranjo on the Nicoya Peninsula. A bus to Nicoya and Santa Cruz meets it. The ship was built in Denmark and has a stormproof lounge, but you can sit out on deck and

165

enjoy the view. You can also ride a boat from behind the market at 9 a.m. (but be there early) on Sundays to San Lucas Island, a prison colony, where the prisoners sell crafts.

The center of town has several pleasant restaurants with good food and a lovely old church. Like Limón, Puntarenas is hot and humid. I think any person from a temperate climate will need a fan or air conditioning that really makes the air move if you take a room not on the waterfront. Accordingly, I did'nt inspect the basic hotels in the center of town used by locals. Ask for a demonstration of the fans or air conditioning.

Along the ocean side of downtown Puntarenas is the Paseo de los Turistas, a tree-lined street and promenade adjoining the beach. There are many soda stands and several hotels. At its far end there's a swimming pool that has been dry for the 2 years I've been there. The beach and water here aren't as clean as in other places, though many people swim. Don't leave anything lying unwatched. Several hotels face this beach and some have very clean pools. You definitely need reservations, especially on weekends.

The east or near end of the peninsula if you're coming from San Jose is the Cocal district. There are several deluxe hotels facing the lagoon and perhaps a dozen sets of cabinas facing the ocean, ranging from basic to deluxe. South of the spit is the ICT recreation area at Doña Ana beach, and farther south is the modern port at Caldera where cruise ships dock to give their passengers a day tour in Costa Rica as far as San Jose.

Note that bus service from Puntarenas back to San Jose even a day or two after a holiday can require a 3 hour wait in the sun. I found several other people in line willing to split the cost of a taxi, about $21 a person for 4.

Where To Stay

Note that most hotels on Costa Rica's west coast have high and low season rates, though their definition of the season varies. Most often it's from early December through March.

Discounts may be 10-30% in low season. You can get excellent values in November.

Costa Rica Yacht Club: (Cocal) Private yacht club catering primarily to members of their club and others, even from other countries. Non-member rates are very high for level of facilities. Overlooks marina on lagoon; ocean beach across road.

Los Chalets: (Charcarita) Very attractive separate cabinas for 8 on shaded ground fronting on beach at east end of Puntarenas spit. Ktchen facilities. Shaded sitting area for each cabina. Rate is per cabina, a good value for a group. Recommended.

Colonial: (Cocal) Deluxe hotel adjacent to Porto Bello, overlooking lagoon. Attractive landscaped grounds and shaded parking. Helpful manager. Can arrange boats and fishing. Casino. Desk staff didn't speak English when we were there. No hot water. Recommended.

Porto Bello: (Cocal) Deluxe hotel well landscaped overlooking the lagoon. Excellent food. Has live music on weekends and can arrange boats and fishing. Helpful manager. Recommended.

Cabinas Los Joron: Pleasant, roomy cabinas with 2 single and 1 double bed, refrigerator and sink. Clean thatched open restaurant overlooking waterfront. Ask for demo of air conditioning.

Las Brisas: New hotel near west end of waterfront. Large rooms with desk and table, acoustical tile ceiling, two story building with 4 rooms on ground level. Excellent food. Guarded parking. Hospitable owner. Recommended.

Tioga: Popular hotel downtown. Reservations a must. Price includes American breakfast, the only meal served. Less expensive rooms have cold water only—but that isn't very cold in Puntarenas! Check-out is late, 2 p.m., which may mean you can't get into rooms early in afternoon if coming from San Jose. Don't leave anything visible in car if you park on street! Pool beautiful. Some rooms have ocean view. Recommended.

The Tioga Hotel has a lovely pool.

Cabinas San Isidro: (Cocal) Not inspected, but looks very good. Same ownership as Los Chalets. Less expensive and across back street from beach but has access.

Las Hamacas: On waterfront downtown. Simple rooms less expensive without air conditioning but well lined up with ocean breeze on 2nd floor. Dance floor and bar on 3rd floor are noisy and have speakers going most of day.

There are additional cabinas in the Cocal and Chacarita areas of the west end of the Puntarenas spit, a few hundred meters east of the big hospital. Some are deluxe and others quite basic. Not inspected: **Cabinas Orlando** has a pool and **Villas Palmas** also is attractive. All are much quieter mid-week than on weekends or holidays.

The following hotel is in Esparza, several miles before you get to Puntarenas, near the junction of the Inter-American Highway and the road to Puntarenas, on the south side of the latter.

Esparza

Castañuelas: Altitude a bit higher and cooler than Puntarenas, an option if hotels below are full. Large rooms with table, twin beds, trees set back from highway. Price varies whether room has fan or a.c., both effective. Coffee shops nearby. Good value.

Gulf of Nicoya

Isla Jesusita: On an island in the gulf, reached by public launch or the hotel's own boat. Lodge and cottages, hammocks in shade. Can arrange fishing. Package tours include transportation from San Jose. Not inspected. U.S. toll-free phone: 800-327-9408.

South of Puntarenas

Each village in Costa Rica has at least basic hotels used by the locals. South of Puntarenas more tourist accommodations are being built, on Isla Herradura between Puntarenas and Jacó Beach.

The *costanera* is Costa Rica's priority road project. It's a wide, two-lane road with gentle grades and good gravel where it isn't paved, that now runs from just outside Puntareanas south past Doña Ana beach, Mata Limón, the modern port of Caldera, Playas Tarcoles and Herradura, Carara Biological Reserve, Jacó Beach, Esterillos, Quepos (with its spur road to Manuel Antonio), south across a dozen or more Bailey bridges built in 1987 by U.S. Army engineers as a gift to Costa Rica, to Playa Dominical. Eventually it will be extended, but now the main road cuts inland through the hills to San Isidro de El General on the Inter-American Hwy. We will discuss the resort areas and hotels in the order you'll find them driving south.

Starting from the east end of Puntarenas spit and continuing down the coast almost to Jacó, there are several good surfing beaches with very consistent waves. River mouths with estuaries and mangrove swamps just upstream attract many birds, caymans, and even crocodiles. You can see wood storks, roseate spoonbills, scarlet macaws, and crocodiles up to 12 feet long from the highway if you're lucky and look sharp! Several older

Western Region

	Isla Jesusita	Rio Mar	Casablanca	Manglares	Club Marparaiso	Cabinas Tanyeri	Jacó Beach	Cocal
Price Range		E	F	F	B	B	C	D
Cleanliness		exc	exc	very good	very good	exc	exc	exc
Noise Level	exc	very good	exc	exc	exc	exc	exc	exc
English Spoken	x	x	x		x		x	x
Pool		x			x	x	x	x
On Waterfrnt		x	x	x	x	x	x	x
Tv								
Elevator							x	
Bar			x	x	x		x	x
Restaur't	x	x		x	x		x	x
Parking		x	x	x	x	x	x	x
Air Cond Or Fan	Not Inspected	x		x	x	x	x	x
Courtesy Transp.	x						x	
In Town					x	x	x	x
W/Bath		all	all	all	all	all	all	all
Rooms No. Of		52	13	29	24	10	120	23
Telephone	61-02-63 33-66-64 1-800-327-9408	63-01-58	22-29-21	63-40-10 63-40-13	67-30-25	42-09-77	64-30-64	64-30-67
Address	Apdo. 84 Puntarenas	Boca de Barranca Apdo. 250 Puntarenas	Mata Limón Av 14, Calle 2/4 San Jose, CR	Mata Limón Esparza, Punt.	Apdo. 024 Jacó, Punt.	Jacó Apdo. 622 Alajuela	Apdo. 962 San Jose, CR	Hotel Cocal Playa Jacó, CR
Hotel	GULF OF NICOYA — Isla Jesusita	SOUTH-WEST COAST — Rio Mar	MATA LIMON — Casablanca	Manglares	JACO BEACH — Club Marparaiso	Cabinas Tanyeri	Jacó Beach	Cocal

Price ranges for single room: A+, over $70; A, $54-70; B, $36-54; C, $24-36; D, $14-24; E, $8-14; F, up to $8. Plus 13% tax.

hotels and cabinas offer simple rooms often overlooking the estuaries. By road (car, taxi or bus from Puntarenas) or the electric train, this is a quiet area for budget birdwatching if you avoid weekends and holidays with crowds and tape recorders. At Mata Limón you may be able to rent a boat or pay a local guide with one to take you birding in the mangrove channels.

Rio Mar: Older hotel north of highway. All rooms have shaded sitting area. Room behind, particularly on breezy second floor, look out on mangroves and water. Surfers stay here to use waves at mouth of the Barranca River. Bus between Puntareanas and Quepos will stop at entrance.

Doña Ana Recreation area on your right is a sheltered beach with shade between rocky points. Safe swimming, shaded picnic area with tables. Small soda bar restaurant, dressing rooms. No camping. Admission 25 colones/adult.

Hotel Manglares at Mata Limon.

Mata Limón

Mata Limón was one of Costa Rica's original beach resorts, on an estuary across from the port of Caldera. The village is divided by the river, with entrances to both parts of it from the highway. The north side is also an electric train stop. On the

171

north side there are 2 older hotels and a few houses. A high wooden footbridge (use flashlight at night to avoid missing planks) crosses the river, giving a fine view of the whole area. On the south side is main village with several sets of cabinas, not inspected, and restaurant, **Costa El Sol,** owned by Ringo Lastro, who can answer anything, arranges for boats, guides, etc. (67-40-08). Deep sea fishing available. **Hotel Viña del Mar, Villas Fanny** and **Villas America** look basic but OK.

Ornithologist Paul Slud did some early work here. For those who can live simply, this seems to me a good nature-viewing spot to spend a few days, and an enjoyable excursion using the train at least one way from San Jose. You'd want to avoid holidays and weekends, especially Dec. 15 to Mar. 1.

On the north side, near the train stop, **Cabinas Las Santas** looked good though not inspected. Have cooking facilities. (41-05-10, 41-00-13).

Casablanca: Shaded, basic but with private shower, screens. Overlooking estuary.

Manglares: Screened to catch breeze. Portable fans available. Balcony and open air restaurant overlooking estuary. Dance floor. Adjacent to train stop. Excellent value.

Playa Tarcoles, Herradura

Playa Tarcoles is gravel but calm, near Carara Biological Reserve. Lagoons with birds including storks. I saw 2 scarlet macaws on the 2 km gravel road leading from the highway. **Cabinas Villa del Mar** is a shaded 2 story building, not inspected and not right on the beach. Upper level looks OK. There's at least 1 set of basic cabinas. Camping is OK on the beach, with some shade. Bar, restaurant, ice available.

Playa Herradura is a sheltered black sand beach with safe swimming 3 km from hwy. Several restaurants and bars. Shaded camping along beach. Despite signs about keeping sites clean, there are few trash cans. Be prepared to clean up site initially. One private campground on lawn with trees just back from

Woodstorks catch early morning sun in a tree at Carara.

Woodstorks and roseate spoonbills among water hyacinths beside the costanera.

beach and another about 2 blocks from the beach on the road in.

173

Jacó Beach

This excellent long beach is easily reached from San Jose and can be crowded on weekends and holidays, as the bus goes there and it's only a 3-hour drive from San Jose via Atenas, San Mateo and Orotina on a scenic hilly paved road that joins the costanera just below Orotina. I'm not sure if you would presently save time by driving from San Jose to the outskirts of Puntarenas and turning south on the costanera at its beginning. This route is less scenic, but the road is wider and route simplier.

Jacó Beach has surf enjoyed by board surfers but also has rips that can be strong. Only strong, knowledgable swimmers should swim in the ocean. If you are caught in a rip, which may appear as a muddy streak leading out from shore where the surf is lower, you should not fight it, but swim parallel to shore until you are free of the current and then swim in. Swimmers are lost every year when they exhaust themselves trying to swim to shore against the rip current. Most hotels have pools. Playa Hermosa, a few miles south is well known for surfing with very consistent waves and has been the site of surfing contests.

This resort has restaurant, bars, discos, 2 small grocery stores, and several small camping areas.

Where To Stay

Club Marparaiso: Attractive modern 3 story facing beach. Large rooms have sitting area, sink, 2 double beds (low). Wading pool. Pool table.

Cabinas Tanyerí: Modern buildings well separated, shaded, landscaped, attractive. Rate is per cabina with up to 3 bedrooms, kitchen with 2 burner stove, roofed outside eating area. Pool, pingpong and refreshment area well-separated from rooms.

Jacó Beach Hotel: Deluxe hotel under same ownership as Iraz in San Jose with a courtesy bus from San Jose. Grounds beautifully landscaped adjoining beach. Big, clean pool has island in middle. Large rooms with tub and shower, marble floors and sinks from Guatemala and El Salvador. Newly redecorated wing has elevator, individual balconies facing pool. Suites have refrigerator, sitting room. Good food. Moped rentals.

Cocal: Very pleasant, small hotel on beach south of town. Eight rooms face beach with outside decks. Deluxe dining room. Shaded, breezy sitting area with hammocks in trees, 2 pools. Hotel entirely ground level. German spoken. Recommended.

Cabinas Heredia: Freshly painted. Bunk beds. Rooms screened on side facing landscaped yard. Some have no opening at back so no breeze through. Need fans. OK otherwise. No single rate.

Complejo Turistico Pentagono: Modern 2 story building facing beach. Simple rooms have 2 dbl. beds. Disco at front and restaurant catch breeze well. No single rate.

El Jardin: Shaded sitting beside pool and beach. Attractive, simple rooms. Belgian owner.

Cabinas Las Palmas: Large clean rooms with 1 double bed & 1 single. Lawn and landscaping with barbecue, a block from beach. Many North Americans stay here. Less that $16/cabina for 1 or 2. Simple, cool, clean.

Cabinas Alice: Each simple room has its own shaded sitting area with table. Price quoted is good value. Readers report it may be negotiable upward on weekends.

Cabinas Antonio: Lawn, landscaping, pleasant rooms. Ground level. Shaded sitting area.

Cabinas Playa Las Brisas: Two modern very pleasant bungalows are Range D. Rooms in main unit were being remodeled and may have price increase. Attractive grounds fronting beach. North American owner. Recommended.

At north end of town, **Cabinas Chelo:** has basic cheap cabinas, clean shaded and friendly. Also camping. Not inspected, but look OK if basic. **Cabinas Super Tica** near main road, and **Cabinas Cindy** and **Cabinas El Bohio** on the beach. Near the south end of town, **Tropical Camping** is a private campground

Western Region (cont'd)

	Heredia	Complejo Turístico Pentagono	El Jardin	Cabinas Las Palmas	Cabinas Alice	Cabinas Playa Las Brisas	Cabinas Antonio	Delfin	Cabinas Los Angeles
Address	Playa Jacó, CR	Playa Jacó, CR	Playa Jacó, CR	Apdo. 5 Playa Jacó, CR	Playa Jacó, CR	Apdo. 008 Jacó, CR	Playa Jacó, CR	Playa Esterillos Apdo. 37 Parrita, Punt.	Apdo. 5329 Esterillos, CR
Telephone	64-31-31		64-30-50	64-30-05	64-30-61	64-30-87	64-30-43	71-16-40	22-85-03
Rooms No. Of	12	20	8	14	12	11	11	15	8
W/Bath	all	all	all	all	all	all	all	all	all
In Town	x			x					
Courtesy Transp.									
Air Cond Or Fan			x	x	x	x	x	x	x
Parking		x	x	x	x	x	x	x	x
Restaur't		x	x		x			x	x
Bar		x	x		x			x	x
Elevator									
Tv									
On Waterfrnt		x		x		x	x	x	x
Pool			x	x				x	x
English Spoken			x	x		x		x	
Noise Level	very good	very good	very good	exc	?	?	exc	exc	exc
Cleanliness	exc	exc	exc	exc	?	?	very good	exc	good
Price Range	D	D	D	D	E	E	F	B	C

(Note: Delfin and Cabinas Los Angeles are listed under the sub-heading ESTERILLOS.)

Price ranges for single room: A+, over $70; A, $54-70; B, $36-54; C, $24-36; D, $14-24; E, $8-14; F, up to $8. Plus 13% tax.

facing the beach with showers, picnic tables and palms, inexpensive, but peace depends on crowd.

Esterillos

Esterillos is a seven-mile-long beach with virtually no one on it though it's less than a mile from the main highway. You'll see signs to the west and east ends. Be careful of rips as it's open with surf. Turtles still hatch on beach. All facilities on this beach seem priced high for what is offered, but even at the beginning of semana santa it was quiet.

Esterillos Oeste is the northwest end of the beach, with some surf, but looks OK for strong swimmers or waders. Quiet laid back area with a few houses and 3 sets of cabinas. **Cabinas Caletas** is too basic with bare mattresses and no breeze. About $9 per bare room seemed high. Some camping on lawn with tents. Two more modern sets nearby had no owners present.

Esterillos Este:
El Delfin: Best designed beach hotel building I've seen. Each room with balcony catching every breeze. Secluded, beautiful spot.

Cabinas Los Angeles: Back road parallel to beach, too basic for Range C, no single rate. Rooms filled with 4-6 cots, bare mattresses. Have 2 burner stove.

Cabinas El Pelicano: refused inspection, was partly occupied, where road reaches beach. Basic cabinas.

The road continues south through palm nut plantations and several villages, including Parrita, which has a beach and some basic accommodations. Note that beaches near river mouths, as this is, have some mud in the sea.

Quepos

Quepos was a banana port, but now is a marketing center and gateway to Manuel Antonio resorts and beaches. Daily buses and flights from San Jose reach Quepos while shuttle buses and taxis run regularly the few miles on to Manuel Antonio. Quepos has a beach used mostly by locals, a dock area. Basic accommodations, cantinas, and groceries those cooking for themselves at Manuel Antonio need. A mangrove area at the north end of town has good birdwatching morning and night.

Viña del Mar: Hotel on right side entering Quepos from north. Faces lagoon with another across road. Rooms for 1-5 people, light, airy, with hardwood, but not deluxe.

Quepos: Very clean basic rooms with fans on second floor. Peace Corps members use. Restaurants and night life in town— can use bus to get to park. Good value.

Manuel Antonio

The 3 beaches, separated by headlands, at Manuel Antonio are as beautiful as any in the world . You can drive to the first beach, a long open one with some rip currents that need respect. You wade a creek and walk to the second and third beaches in Manuel Antonio National Park. These are more sheltered and much safer swimming. Camping is allowed among the trees on Second and Third Beaches. Some accommodations are adjacent to first beach and others are on the hills above. You should have reservations during the holidays when many people from San Jose come. The Vela Bar, on a hill above first beach, serves excellent, reasonably priced food, including local seafood, at a fraction of the prices in San Jose.

Especially during holidays, you should be concerned about the safety of your valuables while you swim or leave camp, etc. The park entrance station will sometimes keep a day pack for you. When I've been swimming by myself here, usually on Third Beach, I've left my day pack with friendly family groups camped nearby.

On early morning and late afternoon walks here you may see 3-toed sloths, white-faced or capuchin monkeys, and rare marmoset or squirrel monkey (smallest of the 4 kinds in Costa Rica), as well as many birds. Troops of monkeys often swing through trees in the camping area at Third Beach!

Offshore island at Manuel Antonio.

Where to Stay

Mariposa: On ridge above beach with smashing views from every room including the bathrooms. Luxurious, exclusive. Price includes breakfast and dinner. Adult guests only. North American owned.

La Quinta: On rolling hilltop north of Manuel Antonio, it has deluxe separate cabinas with balconies, fine view, screens and fans. Some have kitchenette. Can serve breakfast. Readers rave. Recommended.

Apartotel Karahe: Cabinas on hill above highway (path down to beach) have daily maid service, cooking facilities, hammock in private area with super view, attractive stone work. Rate is per cabina whether 1 or 2 people. Weekly, monthly rates especially in off season. Manager helpful, fluent English. Recommended.

Cabinas Divisamar: Attractive. Rooms have 2 double beds. Courtesy transportation to beach. Boat tours to offshore islands. Can arrange horses, guide. Does not take credit cards.

179

Cabinas Espadilla: Built in 1987. Large room with 2 dbl and 1 sgl bed.

Cabinas Los Almendros: Comfortable, modern ground-floor rooms with sitting area. In high season, Dec. through Easter, rate is per room. Low season, Range F. Recommended.

La Arboleda: Comfortable, attractive stone cabinas on hillside above beach. Covered sitting area. Monkeys and birds on wooded grounds. Restaurant. Owner hospitable, speaks German. Radios and tape recorders not allowed to disturb peace!

Cabinas Manuel Antonio: Simple rooms with bunk beds, single story with sitting area in front on beach. Very good value for 4-5 people per cabinas. Adjacent to national park at end of road. Popular with young set.

Hotel Manuel Antonio: Pleasant, airy rooms. Upstairs balcony and lounge, not deluxe but nice use of wood. At end of road next to park, so handy to better swimming beaches.

Plinio: On hill north of beach. Porch with hammocks and view over beach. Well known for food and music. Friendly place attracts young international group. Rooms simple, pleasant.

Vela Bar: Large cool rooms in Spanish style on hill above First Beach. In hot season, March and April, these were the coolest rooms at Manuel Antonio. Shaded porch with hammock. Hospitable manager. Excellent food. Recommended.

Cabinas Ramirez: Formerly called Mar y Sombra. Pleasant, ground-level rooms, some on beach, some in building behind. Price higher with fans which most people will need. Shaded sitting area for each room and on grounds fronting beach.

Cabinas Pedro Miguel: Basic, clean, quiet rooms with effective fan on top of hill before reaching Manuel Antonio.

Costa Linda: Basic simple rooms, screened but without fans. Friendly place.

	Viña del Mar	Quepos	Mariposa	La Quinta	Apartotel Karahe	Cabin Divisamar	Cabinas Espadillas	Cabinas Los Almendros	La Arboleda	Cabinas Manuel Antonio
Region	Quepos	Quepos	MANUEL ANTONIO							
Price Range	D	F	A	B	C	D	D	D	D	D
Cleanliness	exc	exc	exc	exc	exc	exc	exc	exc	exc	very good
Noise Level	very good	very good	exc	exc	exc	exc	exc	exc	exc	exc
English Spoken			x	x	x	x				
Pool			x	x						
On Waterfrnt	x								x	x
Tv										
Elevator										
Bar	x		x		x	x		x	x	
Restaur't	x		x	x	x	x		x	x	
Parking	x	x	x	x	x	x	x	x	x	
Air Cond Or Fan	x	x	x		x	x	x	x	x	
Courtesy Transp.										
In Town	x									
W/Bath	all	13	all	all	all	all	all	all	all	all
Rooms No. Of	20	22	10	3	10	9	16	15	22	18
Telephone	77-00-77	77-02-74	77-03-55 1-800-223-6510	77-04-34	77-01-70	25-07-85 77-03-71	77-04-16	77-02-25	77-04-14	77-02-12
Address	Quepos Apdo. 5527 San Jose, CR	Facing Plaza Apdo. 79 Quepos, CR	Apdo. 4 Quepos, CR	Apdo. 76 Quepos, CR	Apdo. 100 Quepos, CR	Apdo. 7857 San Jose, CR	Playa Manuel Antonio	Apdo. 68 Quepos, CR	Apdo. 55 Quepos, CR	Quepos, CR

Price ranges for single room: A+, over $70; A, $54-70; B, $36-54; C, $24-36; D, $14-24; E, $8-14; F, up to $8. Plus 13% tax.

Ranch hands ride into Uvita for supplies.

Bailey bridge built in 1987 by U.S. Army Engineers on the costanera.

Bungalows: Bamboo huts in front of Cabinas Ramirez on beach with 2 bunks. Small, very basic shelter with showers, etc. in separate building. About $1/day.

For rustic living away from it all on a quiet cove just north of Manuel Antonio, you can call Barry Biesanz in Escazú, 28-18-11. He has 2 cabins with a caretaker and reports monkeys and good snorkeling. We did not inspect. If you can reserve them and live primitively, this is one way to beat the crowds on weekends.

Playa Dominical

South of Quepos and 36 km west of San Isidro, this long beach is suitable for swimming only at low tide, but is never crowded.

Cabinas Punta Dominical: Separate, very attractive wood cabinas with balcony and smashing view from cliff-top over beach. Great spot to read or write, with good breeze. Bar, restaurant, fishing, horseback riding. Good value. Recommended.

There are other basic accommodations in the village just north but we didn't inspect.

Golfito

Golfito, I think, has been badly underrated by others as simply a hot sticky banana port. It's a small town on the narrow strip several miles long, between a jungle-covered cliff and the Golfo Dulce, across from the Osa Peninsula. Near banana docks at the north end of town, the flat area widens out into the land-scaped banana company housing, a mangrove lagoon, and the airport and golf course. Birdwatching in and around town is excellent. You can walk up a road on top of the ridge. Most hotels can arrange boats, fishing, snorkling, or visits to nearby fincas with wildlife. As the banana company land is converted to palm plantations requiring less labor, unemployment has risen and many people are struggling. Some North Americans live in the area, owning hotels and fincas.

Part of downtown Golfito from air, showing road leading up ridge starting at the soccer field.

A good gravel road leads up from the first soccer field about 7 km to a microwave station on the ridge above town. High enough to be cooler than town, and covered with flowering trees, vines, and tree ferns, the ridge offers beautiful views over the gulf and south to coastal bays and islands. Many birds, including toucans, live in this forest. If you don't want to hike up from town, a taxi could give you a tour up there and, if you like, drop you off to hike back down whatever distance you choose. The early morning quiet breeze and bird calls are unforgettable.

Roads are good to Golfito. It's a 7-hour bus ride over the scenic Talamanca Mountains on the Inter-American Highway or a half-hour flight on SANSA. While Golfito is not a primary destination, if you have time, a 2 to 5-day trip here is fun and adds another dimension to what you'll see of Costa Rica. The climate is humid and you'll probably want a fan at night. There are comfortable but no deluxe hotels in town.

An air taxi operates out of Golfito providing the shortest air charters into Corcovado National Park. A ferry runs from town

Huge tree ferns line road above Golfito.

to the Osa Peninsula at Puerto Jimenez, which has several basic cabinas, but getting to the park from there involves hitchhiking plus 2 days of hot humid hiking uphill or around the south end of beaches. Chartered skiffs to the park running around the peninsula from the outside have to go over the Sierpe River bar, a dangerous spot unless the tide is right and the operator skillful. Flying into the park in a chartered plane, and going in via Phantom Island Lodge or Marenco Biological Station on the north side of the Osa Peninsula are still your best choices in access.

Where To Stay

Cabinas Playa Tortuga: Very pleasant landscaped grounds with orchids overlooking bay. Cabinas have small patio. Excellent restaurant. Best in town and a good value. Recommended.

Gran Hotel Miramar: Hotel is being renovated, has smaller basic rooms upstairs without fan. Laundry service. Launch available to charter for touring, scuba, fishing. On waterfront. Caters to visiting yachts & can arrange fuel, provide anchorage. North American owned.

Quepos (cont'd)

Hotel	Address	Telephone	Rooms No. Of	W/Bath	In Town	Courtesy Transp.	Air Cond Or Fan	Parking	Restaur't	Bar	Elevator	Tv	On Waterfrnt	Pool	English Spoken	Noise Level	Cleanliness	Price Range
Manuel Antonio	Apdo. 88 Quepos	77-02-90	5	all			x	x	x	x						very good	exc	D
Plinio	1 km from Quepos Apdo. 71 Quepos	77-00-55	6	all			x	x	x	x					x	?	?	D
Vela Bar	Apdo. 13 Quepos	77-04-13	6	all			x	x	x	x					x	exc	exc	C
Cabinas Ramirez	Playas de Manuel Antonio	77-05-10 / 77-00-03	16	all			x	x								exc	?	F
Cabinas Pedro Miquel	km 1 Carretara Manuel Antonio Quepos	77-00-35	5	all			x	x						x		exc	exc	F
Costa Linda	Playa Manuel Antonio Apdo 62, Quepos	77-03-07	11	2				x	x						x	exc	exc	F
PLAYA DOMINICAL Cabinas Dominical	Playa Dominical Apdo. 176 8000 San Isidro de el General, CR	71-08-66 / 25-53-28	4	all			x	x	x	x			x			exc	exc	D
GOLFITO Cabinas Playa Tortuga	Golfito Apdo. 12, Golfito	75-00-62	8	all	x		x	x	x	x			x		x	exc	exc	E
Miramar	Apdo. 60 Golfito	75-01-43	35	all	x		x	x	x	x			x		x	very good	exc	E
Costa Rica Surf	Apdo. 7 Golfito	77-00-34	15	all	x		x	x	x	x			x		x	very good	good	F
Delfina	Golfito	75-00-43	26	7	x		x	x					x			good	very good	F
Golfito	Golfito	75-00-47	16	all	x		x	x	x				x			very good	exc	F

Price ranges for single room: A+, over $70; A, $54-70; B, $36-54; C, $24-36; D, $14-24; E, $8-14; F, up to $8. Plus 13% tax.

Costa Rica Surf: On right side above central district. Some rooms have skylight instead of windows. Upstairs lounge. North American owned. Can arrange surfing, nature trips, snorkeling, fill air tanks.

Cabinas Delfina: Two styles—basic rooms with partitions not all the way up, no bath. More modern rooms with bath (cold water), ones facing away from street are quiet.

Golfito: On left halfway through town. Gov't employees stay here. Waterfront rooms preferred. Restaurant manager speaks English. Can take guests to her small farm with capuchin monkeys, etc. Good value. Recommended.

In Golfito checkout times are before noon because no one has dryers and sheets are expensive, so they must be washed and have time to dry before the afternoon rain!

Brown pelicans.

187

Marenco Biological Station.

Hauling the baggage up to Marenco.

In the wheelhouse of the Puntarenas ferry.

Northwest Region
(Nicoya Peninsula, Guanacaste, Monteverde)

This region has the majority of Costa Rica's beach resorts, several of its volcanoes, and the biological preserve of Monteverde. Access by air is to many small resort strips or the regional airport at Liberia. Ferries cross the Gulf of Nicoya from Puntarenas and shuttle many times a day across the head of the gulf near the mouth of the Tempisque River. The Inter-American Highway runs from San Jose down to the western coastal plain and northward through Liberia to the Nicaraguan border.

A good two-lane road, mostly paved. leads from the Puntarenas ferry terminal through Jicaral, Nicoya, and Santa Cruz to Liberia. A bus meets the ferry and runs north, though one usually changes buses at Santa Cruz. Smaller roads, some of them 4-wheel-drive all year and some only during the wet season, run from these towns out to the coast. All-weather roads run with bus service to Playas Tamarindo and Coco. While there's daily bus service to Nosara and Sámara, it can be an adventure in the wet season. Some of these buses go to the coast and stay overnight, coming back the next day. Their main purpose is to let the coastal people come to town to shop. It's a fascinating area, and bus riding is one way to see it cheaply. Some resorts have transportation all the way from San José, while others will pick you up at the local airstrip or at the Liberia airport. If there are several of you, or you're going to be on the coast for some days, a taxi ride from Liberia or Santa Cruz may be quite reasonable.

Santa Cruz, Nicoya and Liberia have festivals, rodeos and bullfights that are worth a trip from San José or a day in town from the beach. Remember that in Costa Rican bullfights, the bull chases the people around and isn't killed. When festivals are happening, you'll need hotel reservations, and your best chance of getting them is in Liberia, where there are a number of large reasonably-priced hotels. At presstime, no one has yet put a tour or car rental agency (and we've heard one is planned) in Liberia, though it's centrally located for a wide range of interesting day trips to mountains, beaches, rodeos, and national parks.

Guanacaste is the driest part of Costa Rica and most cattle land is burned off during the dry season, producing smoke and dust, particularly in March and April. The rainy season, however, isn't very rainy here, and I especially like November, when the grass is green, hotels still have off-season rates, there are no crowds, and the frequent high overcast limits heat and sunburn (a little).

ICT is promoting more road signs and paving to tourist areas, but particularly around Sámara, Garza, and Nosara, the dirt tracks are presently quite anonymous and easy to get lost on especially after dark. Do fill a car with gas in the main towns as most of the beach resorts don't have service stations.

Practically every village in the country has basic rooms or basic hotels at rock-bottom prices, generally cleaner than you'd expect from the outside, but frequently at a lower level than you'll want unless you're on a bare survival budget. There are some of the "we'd rather sleep on the beach" sort, though few of those are listed here. I stayed in one at Nosara when daylight ran out and there was a closed hotel to inspect the next day. The room was clean, but I had to be careful not to trip over the black pig in the backyard en route to the privy in the dark! Costa Rica has hundreds of hotels far above that level, but it has the full range.

On the coast, you'll want a building carefully aligned with the prevailing breeze or a fan, often more comfortable than air conditioning, and considerably more common. Starting with the southern end of the Nicoya Peninsula, actually in Puntarenas province, we'll work our way generally north, covering Lake Arenal and Monteverde on the way back to San Jose. Remember the 20-30% low season discounts offered by most hotels.

Where To Stay

Oasis del Pacifica: On your left as the ferry from Puntarenas nears the dock. Very attractive, landscaped grounds facing gravel beach with shells. Waterfront bar with music, dancing. Screened open-air dining room, thatched shelters with hammocks, large clean pool, wading pool, tennis. Adjacent woods for bird-watchers, horses, fishing.

De Paso: on road leading away from terminal. Day tours to nearby beaches. Service outstanding. Recommended.

Bahia Gigante: Large rooms with dbl and sgl beds in each. Shaded walk with hammocks. Inland from shore on road from ferry to Tambor.

Playa Tambor is a calm black sand beach with safe swimming on the south coast of the Nicoya Peninsula. You can drive from the Puntarenas ferry on good gravel road or ride the bus that meets the Paquera ferry and goes to Cóbano. Charter planes land on the lawn airstrip at the hacienda. With only 2 hotels, this is a quiet area anytime.

Hacienda La Tambor: Deluxe hotel in rustic style on working cattle ranch. Shaded veranda overlooks corrals. Beautifully landscaped grounds with some thatched bungalows besides rooms. Attractive pool. Excellent food. Recommended.

Dos Logartos: Rustic, simple hotel on landscaped grounds fronting beach. Rooms with bath. Range E.

The south Nicoya coast from Montezuma to Cabo Blanco.

Playa Montezuma is a group of Costa Rica's finest beaches, reachable by taxi from the bus at Cóbano or by car. This is as far as you should go with 2-wheel drive. You can walk or ride rental horses along the beaches in either direction, even as far as Cabo Blanco Biological Reserve, about 5 miles west, which you need advance permission from the Park Service to enter. Good snorkeling in rocky coves west of the village. About half a mile west of the village, the road crosses a creek worth walking up to see a very pretty waterfall. Do watch for snakes—we saw a fer-de-lance run over on the road though we didn't see any in the woods.

Nicoya Peninsula

Hotel	Price Range	Cleanliness	Noise Level	English Spoken	Pool	On Waterfrnt	Tv	Elevator	Bar	Restaur't	Parking	Air Cond Or Fan	Courtesy Transp.	In Town	W/Bath	Rooms No. Of	Telephone	Address
PLAYA NARANJO																		
Oasis del Pacifico	D	very good	exc	×	×	×			×	×	×	×	×		all	36	61-15-55	Apdo. 200 Puntarenas
De Paso	E	exc	exc	×	×				×	×	×	×	×		all	14	61-26-10	Apdo. 2320/2120 Calle Blanco
Bahia Gigante	C	very good	very good		×				×	×	×	×			all	9	61-24-42	Bahia Gigante
PLAYA TAMBOR																		
Hacienda Tambor	B	exc	exc	×	×	×			×	×	×	×	×	×	all	26	61-29-80	Apdo. 398 San Pedro Montes de Oca
Dos Logartos	F	exc	very good			×				×	×	×		×	4	24	61-11-22	Tambor de Puntarenas
PLAYA MONTEZUMA																		
Cabinas Mar y Cielo	F	exc	very good	×		×			×	×	×	×		×	all	8 + house	61-24-72	Playa Montezuma 536 Cobano, Punt.
Montezuma	F	exc	very good	×					×	×	×	×	×	×	9	18	61-24-72	Playa Montezuma Montezuma de Cóbano, Punt.
JICARAL																		
Guamalé	F	very good	exc						×	×	×	×		×	6	13	64-00-73	Jicaral Puntarenas
NICOYA																		
Curime	C	very good	exc		×				×	×	×	×			all	20	68-52-38	Apdo. 51 Nicoya
Jenny	E	exc	exc								×	×		×	all	24	68-50-50	50 N. Repetidora Columbia, Nicoya
Cabinas Loma Bonita	F	very good	very good						×	×	×	×		×	all	11	68-52-69	Frente de Hosp. Nicoya
Chorotega	F	exc	exc									×		×	all	24	68-52-45	Hotel al Norte Chorotega Nicoya
Las Tinajas	F	exc	exc							×	×	×		×	all	20	68-50-81	Hotel las Tinajas Nicoya

Price ranges for single room: A+, over $70; A, $54-70; B, $36-54; C, $24-36; D, $14-24; E, $8-14; F, up to $8. Plus 13% tax.

If you see children carrying live lobsters and fresh-caught fish in from that direction, you might follow along to see which restaurant buys them while you decide where to have dinner! The lobster dinner we had at Chico's Bar and Restaurant (location of the village's only phone, 61-24-72) was great. At presstime there's 1 hotel and 3 sets of cabinas were being built. It's a long way, but holidays can be busy here. Using the phone you can reserve rooms at the hotel and cabinas listed. The other 2 more basic cabinas are less than 100 yards uphill, but not reachable by phone and no owners were there so we didn't inspect.

Cabinas Mar y Cielo: Attractive rooms with balcony and shaded sitting area. Rooms have 1 dbl and several sgl beds. Ask for upstairs rooms for most breeze. Recommended.

Hotel Montezuma: Upper level sitting area with hammocks. Most rooms have 1 dbl and several sgl beds. Portable fans. Get room on ocean side for breeze. Not as quiet as cabinas, but OK.

Drug running plane from Panama crash-landed on the beach near Montezuma. As long as North America buys, this will continue.

Passengers and produce going to Puntarenas market fill the Paquera launch.

Mal País is about as far as you can go in Costa Rica, 4-wheel drive most of the year from Cóbano due to a stream crossing. It's a village with a miles-long light sand beach and surf running north from Cabo Blanco. There is presently no access from that side to the reserve. You could probably arrange to stay with someone in the village and could rent horses, but there were no tourist facilities when we visited. Several people talked of building them. Otto Angulo, owner of a soda bar, would be a good man to ask.

From here we go back to the main road above the Puntarenas ferry and go north toward Nicoya.

Guamalé: In village of Jicaral, first village north of ferry. Not resort area, but you could need a night here to make ferry schedule. Clean, with cold water, and has small, clean tipico restaurant.

195

Calypso's passengers head for shore and lunch, some by boat and some swimming.

Nicoya

Nicoya is a government and marketing center for the southern peninsula and has a colonial church downtown.

Where To Stay

Curime: The only resort level hotel in town is actually a set of cabinas for 4 on landscaped grounds outside of town—very well done. Each has 2 single and 1 double bed, sitting room, bar, refrigerator. Rate is for each cabina. Large pool. TV.

Cabinas Loma Bonita: As you enter Nicoya, on left, above level of road. Shaded parking. Basic but may be quietest in town.

Jenny: Large open style. TV in rooms; cold water, but very good value. Fenced parking. Ask for demo of air conditioning.

Chorotega: Simple rooms with tile floors. Back rooms open to court, light and airy. Good value at this level.

Las Tinajas: Rooms larger than most. Quieter at back away from bus station. Enclosed parking behind. Manager speaks no English, but friendly. Recommended at this level.

Sámara, Garza, and Nosara

These are 3 beautiful, light sand beaches reached from Nicoya. The villages of Sámara and Garza are at the beaches, while Nosara is inland. All are rather basic coastal villages without a resort atmosphere, though near Nosara there's a real estate development with many retired North Americans. The beaches have gentle surf and headlands at the ends. Fishing and boating aren't immediately obvious here, though a Garza boatbuilder builds fishing boats beside the road. Sámara and Nosara have very basic accommodations in town, but all have some tourist facilities outside. If you're avoiding crowds during holidays and make reservations for the limited tourist rooms, or camp, these would be a good choice. There's daily bus service from Nicoya though the road may be impassable in rainy season. Don't count on being able to drive north from Nosara in the wet season even with 4-wheel-drive. Ask the locals about road conditions.

Playa Sámara has a reef offshore so waves are small and swimming safe. Beach is white sand.

Las Brisas del Pacifico: Very attractive hotel with pool fronting beach. Large rooms with high ceilings, nice woodwork. Shaded sitting area for each cabina. No single rate. Children to 14 free in same room. Hospitable German manager. Can arrange surfing, diving, horses, jet skiing. Recommended.

Cabinas Punta Sámara: Very basic budget rooms. There's another set nearby, in village.

Near Garza:
Villaggio La Guaria Morada: Deluxe cabinas and resort with swimming pool, horseback riding, deep-sea fishing, and snorkeling. Big rooms, 2 per separate building, but no fans or screens—they depend on breeze. Shaded sitting area.

At Playa Nosara:
Playa Nosara: Attractive cabinas on ridge overlooking beach. Rate for single and double is same (per cabina) Tennis. Fishing. Snorkeling. Landscaping planned to attract birds. Recommended.

Nicoya (2)

PLAYAS SAMARA, GARZA, NOSARA / PLAYA JUNQUILLAL / PLAYA TAMARINDO

Hotel	Address	Telephone	Price Range	Cleanliness	Noise Level	English Spoken	Pool	On Waterfrnt	Tv	Elevator	Bar	Restaur't	Parking	Air Cond Or Fan	Courtesy Transp.	In Town	W/Bath	Rooms No. Of
Las Brisas del Pacifico	Playa Sámara, Apdo. 709, Heredia	68-08-76, 28-09-71	C	good	exc		x	x			x	x	x				all	12
Cabinas Punta Sámara	Congrejal de Sámara	68-00-22	F	fair	high			x			x	x	x	x		x	all	10
Villa Guaria Morada	Garza, Apdo. 860, Centro Colón, Telex 3185 Guione, CR	22-40-73, 68-07-84	B	exc	exc		x	x			x	x	x				all	30
Playas de Nosara	Nosara, Apdo. 53, Boca de Nosara	68-04-95	C	exc	exc	x					x	x	x	x	x		all	16
PLAYA JUNQUILLAL																		
Villa Serena	Apdo. 17, Santa Cruz	68-07-37, 31-50-43	C	exc	exc	x	x	x			x	x	x	x	x		all	6
Autumalal	Apdo. 49, Santa Cruz	68-05-06	C	exc	exc	x	x	x			x	x	x	x			all	20
Playa Junquillal	Apdo. 17, Santa Cruz	68-04-65	E	very good	exc			x			x	x	x	x			all	4
PLAYA TAMARINDO																		
Tamarindo Diriá	Apdo. 21, Santa Cruz	68-06-82	B	exc	exc	x	x	x			x	x	x	x	x	x	all	54
Cabinas Pozo Azúl	Playa Tamarindo, Via Real, Santa Cruz	68-01-47	D	exc	exc		x						x	x		x	all	30
Cabinas Zully Mar	Playas de Tamarindo, Santa Cruz	26-47-32	F	exc	exc							x	x	x		x	all	20
Doly	Playa Tamarindo, Santa Cruz	68-01-74	F	exc	exc			x			x	x	x	x		x	6	12

Price ranges for single room: A+, over $70; A, $54-70; B, $36-54; C, $24-36; D, $14-24; E, $8-14; F, up to $8. Plus 13% tax.

Hotel Nosara overlooks the ocean.

Playa Junquillal

Surf is usually up at this beach when I inspected. Swimming requires caution for rips though long scenic beach would be good walking or riding. Locals catch big fish from rocks on point. Camping is OK on north part of beach and would be improved with some shade. There are 2 deluxe hotels and one set of cabinas here, with no village actually at beach. Access is from Santa Cruz or by flying into strip at Playa Tamarindo to north. It's hard to imagine this area crowded!

Villa Serena: Price includes meals, tennis and equipment. VCR films. Children allowed if parents are responsible for them. Popular as honeymoon spot. No snorkeling, some body-surfing. Large rooms. Dining on balcony overlooking beach and landscaped grounds. May not take singles during high season Dec.-April with limited room. Recommends watching villagers fish from rocks or boat on the point.

199

Hotel Autumalal: Open all year with high season Dec.-Mar. Deluxe duplex cabinas, brick floors, good beds. Thatched roof over dining room on terrace. Rate includes meals. Attractive pool. Fishing, tennis, horses. Wild monkeys live nearby and are seen on the grounds. In trees at south end of beach.

Hotel Playa Junquillal: Is actually 4 cabinas, U.S. owned, fairly basic. Closed and owners unsure if would reopen.

Playa Tamarindo

Playa Tamarindo is 1 of only 2 Guanacaste beaches easily reached at present by public bus and all-year roads from San Jose (the other is Playa Coco) with a full price range of accommodations. These beaches do have a resort atmosphere, food and drink stands, and sometimes crowds and litter. (Fortunately, the price of imported bottles saves Costa Rica from broken glass, as the bottle being worth more than its contents usually means you have to drink it where you get it.)

The swimming is excellent in front of both villages, and there's good snorkeling within walking distance. Tamarindo is famous for deep-sea fishing for sailfish and marlin. Seafood is excellent in restaurants here. Besides bus and car, you can fly via SANSA Monday and Friday from San Jose to the Tamarindo strip.

Tamarindo Diria: Deluxe hotel very well done, no seasonal rates. Game room with pool table, foosball. Landscaped, shaded terrace between pool and ocean. Suites, with sitting room, refrigerator, bar, double and 1 single bed. Our readers recommend.

Cabinas Pozo Azúl: Modern cabinas on left of road as you enter resort. Large light rooms with shaded sitting area in front. Across road from mangroves, beach and river. No single rate.

Cabinas Zully Mar: Comfortable large rooms with tile floors. Less than 100 yds. to ocean, restaurant and bar nearby. Rooms have individually carved doors illustrating Costa Rican legends. Excellent value.

Salt ponds on Gulf of Nicoya shore.

Doly: Simple, inexpensive rooms, but clean, OK. Ask for room facing beach. On beach and well-aligned for breeze without a.c. Great view. Shaded open air restaurant on ground floor.

Playas Conchal, Brasilito, Flamingo, Potrero, Pan de Azucar

North of Tamarindo, across lagoon and river mouth is Brasilito, a small village back from a beautiful beach which would be some of the nicest beach camping anywhere. If you go through Brasilito onto its beach and half a mile south (4-wheel drive at low tide, or walk), you'll reach Conchal, a sheltered white sand and shell beach surrounded by cattle fincas. There's camping under the trees there and water available from the local ranch hands, some of whose children can be paid to watch your gear if you leave camp. The trees are great for hanging hammocks. You'll want a tent to keep out crawlies at night. Snorkeling is good and swimming safe.

Brasilito has small stores, basic cabinas, and fishermen who sell their catch. Two buses a day come from Santa Cruz or a

201

group can use a cab for about $16 one way. On the hill above Brasilito you'll find the following hotel.

Hacienda Las Palmas: Huge, deluxe suites with great view, cooking facilities, shaded veranda. Satellite TV from U.S. Excellent food. Same management also rents luxurious villas on next headland north.

Flamingo Beach and Flamingo Hotel and Presidential Suites.

Flamingo Beach, north of Brasilito, is somewhat sheltered and usually safe for swimming. If it's rough, just wait for the tide and wind to change. Private airstrip is owned by the development. There's a small marina, the only private one north of Puntarenas, several restaurants, and two hotels under the same ownership. Mangroves behind have caymans and good birdwatching.

Flamingo Beach Hotel and **Presidential Suites:** Luxury suites and hotel on headland overlooking Flamingo Beach. All facilities, including complete kitchens in the suites, large swimming pool. Satellite TV from U.S.

202

Playa Potrero is just to the north with a long sheltered beach and good swimming. Behind is a creek with woods and good bird and monkey watching.

Playa Potrero Trailer Park: 2 apartments and 2 trailers with cooking facilities in well-shaded yard a block from the beach. Have own well and good water. Monthly rates.

Playa Potrero: Pleasant beach hotel with large rooms in local hardwoods. No single rates. Quiet hotel. Can arrange horses, snorkeling, scuba rentals including tank refills, boats with gear, fishing for sailfish, marlin, tuna. Coral reefs outside bay reached by boat.

Pan De Azucar.

Pan de Azucar (Sugar Beach): Dining room on terrace overlooking beach, done with taste. Covered porch in front of cabinas. Attractive, quiet area. No single rate. Recommended.

The cooks at the Tortilla Factory in Santa Cruz make good tipico food in a former airplane hangar.

Santa Cruz

If you've gotten to any of the beaches above, you've probably come through this marketing and cattle town before now—if not, the coastal roads and trails will fail you and you'll have to bounce back to the arterial two-lane highway near Santa Cruz to head out to the coast on another road. As roads are improved and bridges built, other beaches such as Playa Ostional north of Nosara (with huge turtle arribas) will be assessible. Santa Cruz is an attractive town with 2 good hotels and several very basic places. If you come for festival or rodeo, make reservations here or in Liberia as all rooms will be full.

Santa Cruz has a restaurant serving such good cheap food for lunch that it is busy despite being a sooty sheet metal shed 3 stories high, the hangar at the former airport! A dozen women inside make excellent tipico food and breads of all kinds, for less than $1 for lunch. Costa Rican government employees stop off here and U.S. TV crews taken to the Tortilla Factory for lunch at the long tables have raved about both the food and the ethnic experience. You can ask anyone for directions, but it's only a couple of blocks from the main square on a back alley.

Diriá: Very attractive hotel with large clean pool. Landscaping, hanging plants. Best in Santa Cruz and excellent value.

Sharatoga: Cool, attractive with shaded center court, deer, monkey, parrots.

Pension Isabel: Basic, clean.

Playas Coco, Ocotal, Bahia Pez Vela

At Playa Ocotal and the cove just south:
El Ocotal: Deluxe resort done in excellent taste. Rooms in duplex cabinas along steep drive (not for new hip replacements!) with great view. Dining room on hilltop with view in all directions. Tennis, horses, snorkeling, boat rentals, fuel. Have 2 coves & marina. Deep sea fishing is serious sport here.

Bahia Pez Vela.

Bahia Pez Vela: Deluxe small fishing camp for up to 11 deep sea fishing enthusiasts, on small cove just south of Playas Coco

205

Nicoya (3)

PLAYAS BRASILITO, FLAMINGO
PLAYA POTRERO
PLAYA PAN DE AZUCAR
SANTA CRUZ
OCOTAL

Hotel	Address	Telephone	Rooms No. Of	W/Bath	In Town	Courtesy Transp.	Air Cond Or Fan	Parking	Restaur't	Bar	Elevator	Tv	On Waterfrnt	Pool	English Spoken	Noise Level	Cleanliness	Price Range
Las Palmas	Brasilito, Apdo. 10, Santa Cruz	68-05-73	5	all		x	x	x	x	x				x	x	exc	very good	B
Flamingo Beach Hotel, Presidental Suites	Apdo 692, Alajuela	39-15-84	23	all		x	x	x		x			x	x	x	exc	exc	A+
Flamingo Beach Hotel	Apdo. 692, Alajuela	39-15-84	45	all		x	x	x	x	x				x	x	exc	exc	A
Playa Potrero	Apdo. 45, Santa Cruz	68-06-69	10	all			x	x	x	x			x	x	x	exc	very good	D
Playa Potrero Trailer Park	Apdo. 61, Santa Cruz		4	all			x	x							x	exc	exc	E
Pan de Azucar Sugar Beach	Apdo. 66, Santa Cruz	68-09-59	11	all	x	x	x	x	x	x			x	x	x	exc	exc	D
Diria	Apdo. 58, Santa Cruz	68-00-80	30	all	x		x	x	x	x					x	exc	exc	E
Shara?toga	Apdo. 345, Santa Cruz	68-00-11	40	all	x		x									good	very good	E
Pension Isabel	Santa Cruz	68-01-73	22				x	x	x	x					x	exc	good	F
Ocotal	Apdo. 1013, 1002 San Jose, CR	23-42-59 / 67-02-30	16	all		x	x	x	x	x			x		x	exc	exc	A
Bahia Pez Vela	Marina Ocotal, Apdo. 101, Playa de Coco, Guanacaste	67-01-29	6	all		x	x	x	x	x			x		x	exc	good	C

Price ranges for single room: A+, over $70; A, $54-70; B, $36-54; C, $24-36; D, $14-24; E, $8-14; F, up to $8. Plus 13% tax.

and Ocotal. When not occupied by fishermen, this is a very attractive resort with sheltered swimming and snorkeling. Good value. Recommended.

Flor de Itabo bungalows.

At Playa Coco:

Flor de Itabo: Well-done with hardwoods, big bathrooms, pleasant rooms, very attractive pool area. Nice landscaping. Also have 2-story bungalows with cooking facilities. Quiet, well removed from crowds at beach. German spoken. On north side of main road entering town about ½ mile from beach.

Aldea Keystone: 2 and 3 room basic single cabinas with stove, refrigerator, among trees back from beach. Shaded sitting area with hammock. Bring your own linen. North American owner.

Cabinas Chale: Very attractive cabinas in quiet northeastern outskirts of town still have short walk to beach. Rate is per cabina, for 1 or 2. Private walled courts behind cabinas. Very good value. Recommended.

Casino Playa de Coco: Good value with rates varying according to season and whether they face sea. Front rooms facing sea are well worth it. Portable fans for rent (you need them). Ask

Fishing with a throw net.

A Costa Rican family plays in a tidepool at Playa Montezuma.

for rooms at far end away from bar. Food good.

Cabinas Luna Tica: Rooms for 4 or 6, not properly aligned to catch breeze. Too basic.

Playa Hermosa

Playa Hermosa is a fine curved beach several miles long just north of Playa del Coco, with good swimming, and deep sea fishing and water sports available. There are 2 widely differing hotels at opposite ends of the beach—you can definitely pick your style here. Aqua Sport, near north end, rents just about any gear you might want and can arrange boats and guides to dive or fish off the Isles Murciélago. There's a bus from Liberia twice a day.

Condovac La Costa: Large group of condos with unoccupied rooms available for rent. Kitchen facilities. Scuba, fishing, water skiing, horses, tennis, discotheque. Golf carts transport guests to rooms. Blanco Travel provides trnasportation from San Jose.

Cabinas Playa Hermosa: Small attractive hotel among the trees just behind the beach. Owned by former Oregon couple who say "We sell tranquility." Does considerable repeat business. Guests can visit the other end of the beach for water sports or an evening out.

Los Corales is a group of new block cabinas just below Condovac. Under construction in 1987 and not able to be inspected. Needs shade.

Playa Panama

Beaches are increasingly sheltered by Punta Mala as you head north here so surf is gone and water calm. ICT has major plans in this area with the Papagayo Project to encourage tourist development and take advantage of maximum good weather. Due to cost, most results are years off. There's a basic shelter and pulpería where the road reaches the shore here, in an otherwise rural area.

Pension Los Bananos: Was not inspected as there weren't any clear signs amid the dirt roads. It's reported to be good and is probably just north of the pulpería above the shore.

Beef cattle in the tropics are usually Cebu, a breed from India.

Liberia
(pop. 14,800)

Liberia is the provincial capital of Guanacaste, a clean, busy town on the Inter-American Highway at its junction with the road to Santa Cruz and Nicoya. As I previously mentioned, it has excellent, reasonably-priced hotels, mostly with large cool swimming pools you'll appreciate in the heat, and an amazing variety of interesting day trips available if you have transportation. Most can be reached by bus, but the round trip isn't practical in a day with current bus schedules. There are several buses daily between Liberia and San Jose. From Liberia you can drive to northern Guanacaste beaches, Santa Rosa and Rincon de la Vieja National Parks, Lake Arenal and Arenal Volcano with moving lava flows, Barra Honda and Palo Verde National Parks, and festivals at Nicoya and Santa Cruz, returning to Liberia at night. I've found Liberia a good overnight spot to rest and clean up between camping trips to parks and beaches.

The casona at Santa Rosa where William Walker and his men were surrounded.

Bats sleep through the day in a corner of Santa Rosa's museum.

Where To Stay

Las Espuelas: Very attractive hotel with entrance shaded by huge guanacaste tree. Interior courts with ponds and pre-Columbian figures. Planted breezeways, hardwood furniture in Spanish colonial style. Season discount close to 50%. Conference room. Wheelchair accessible. Central air conditioning. Very helpful manager with some English. Highly recommended.

El Sitio: Large attractive hotel with architecture, decoration and planting all in Guanacaste cattle country theme. Wheelchair ramp even for 3 steps from lobby to pool level. Rooms without a.c. are oriented to breeze. Recommended. Low season rates and honeymoon discount.

Nuevo Boyeros: Big clean 2-story hotel around court with large clean swimming pool and wading pool with cascade. Cool rooms with good beds. Small restaurant serves good food, super fruit refrescos. Popular with truckdrivers and government employees. Dance floor in front. On weekends ask for room at back for quiet. Good value. Recommended.

Hotel Bramadero: Shaded sitting area with distinctive Nicaraguan rocking chairs. All rooms now have fans or a.c. Pool filled and clean. Restaurant reported good.

La Ronda: Named for round dining room on second floor with good breeze. Rooms big with tile floors. Pool small. Hot water. Ask for demo of air conditioning..

La Siesta: Small, modern, pleasant hotel with good beds downtown. Second floor rooms bigger, worth asking for. Small clean pool. Manager helpful.

Oriental: Very basic. Chinese operated. Rooms without a.c. very hot. Ask for demo of a.c. to be sure it's effective.

Nicoya (4)

	Flor de Itabo	Aldea Keystone	Cabinas Chale	Casino Playa de Coco	Cabinas Luna Tica	Condovac	Cabinas Playa Hermosa	Los Corales	Las Espuelas	El Sitio	Nuevo Boyeros	Bramadero
Price Range	B	C	D	F	F	B	D		C	E	E	F
Cleanliness	good	very good	exc	very good	very good	exc	exc		exc	exc	exc	very good
Noise Level	exc	exc	exc	good	poor	exc	exc	exc	exc	exc	exc	very good
English Spoken						x	x		x			
Pool	x		x			x			x	x	x	x
On Waterfrnt				x			x					
Tv								under construction	x			
Elevator												
Bar	x		x	x	x	x	x		x	x	x	x
Restaur't	x		x	x	x	x	x		x	x	x	x
Parking	x	x	x	x	x	x	x	x	x	x	x	x
Air Cond Or Fan	x		x	x	x	x	x		x	x	x	x
Courtesy Transp.	x					x			x			
In Town		x		x					x		x	x
W/Bath	all	all	all	all	all	all	all		all	all	all	all
Rooms No. Of	13	7	18	75	17	100	20	90	41	52	60	25
Telephone	67-00-11	32-02-10	67-01-67	67-01-27	67-02-67	67-01-36			66-01-44 TELEX SPUR CR 6502	66-12-11	66-07-22	66-03-71
Address	Apdo. 32 Carillo, Guanacaste	Apdo. 10 Playa de Coco	Playa de Coco	Apdo. 2y3 Carillo, Guanacaste	Playa de Coco	Apdo. 55 BGB San Jose, CR	Apdo. 112 Liberia, Guanacaste	Inter Amer., Hwy	Apdo. 88 Liberia	Apdo. 134 Liberia	Inter Amer., Hwy. Apdo. 85 Liberia	I-A Hwy. & Santa Cruz Apdo. 70 Liberia

Section headings within the Hotel column: PLAYA DE COCO (Flor de Itabo, Aldea Keystone, Cabinas Chale, Casino Playa de Coco, Cabinas Luna Tica); PLAYA HERMOSA (Condovac, Cabinas Playa Hermosa); LIBERIA (Los Corales, Las Espuelas, El Sitio, Nuevo Boyeros, Bramadero).

Price ranges for single room: A+, over $70; A, $54-70; B, $36-54; C, $24-36; D, $14-24; E, $8-14; F, up to $8. Plus 13% tax.

Bare-throated tiger bittern at Palo Verde.

Wildlife is where you find it. 5 woodstorks feed in pond beside highway and barrio in Puntarenas.

Cañas

Cañas, on the Inter-American Highway, marks the turnoff to Tilarán and Lake Arenal. While not as cool as Tilarán, it's a central spot for trips to Arenal and the nearest good base for birdwatching in Palo Verde National Park and the Gulf of Nicoya.

Hacienda La Pacifica: Older, hardwood cabinas and new, well-designed units. Both good value. Swiss food. New tiled pool. Wildlife and the Bebedero River on premises. It's possible to float the river on rafts from here to Bebedero or all the way to the gulf. Horses available to ride on adjacent hacienda. 5 km. north of Cañas on high way. Recommended.

Tilarán

This small town is high on hills above Guanacaste plain, near Lake Arenal. It's clean, with a cool breeze, and has several restaurants with good tipico food. The country around the lake is lovely rolling upland with dairy cattle, and the lake is famous for fishing. Afternoon breezes across the lake can be very strong. Boats and fishing can be arranged though Tilarán doesn't seem touristy and all I met spoke only Spanish. Has fiesta in April with rodeo and livestock show.

Where To Stay

Cabinas El Sueño: Light, airy, small hotel with rooms arranged around central court with fountain on second floor. Hot water. Manager very pleasant. Recommended. Restaurant below makes great ceviche and good refrescos.

Cabinas Mary: Hotel is upstairs, light airy, friendly, TV in living room. Excellent value. Hint: tall people should duck when going upstairs.

Cabinas Naralit: Small rooms on ground floor, but light, pleasant. Bar next door may be noisy on weekend.

Central: Rooms on 1st and 2nd floors, back from street. Good value.

Fountain upstairs at Tilaran's El Sueno

Monteverde

Monteverde isn't a national park; it's a biological reserve administered by the Tropical Science Center in San Jose. However, for nature lovers it's a major destination, as anyone who watches international nature programs on TV knows.

A group of Quakers from the United States and other countries founded a colony, choosing Costa Rica for its peace and tolerance. Today they and their decendants raise dairy cattle and goats on the steep slopes above the village of Santa Elena. Their cooperative makes very fine cheeses sold locally and in San Jose. Artistic members paint Christmas cards, calendars, and other products. The colony is at the bottom edge of the cloud forest, far from tropical heat—and at the end of a long winding road up from the Inter-American Highway (bus daily from Puntarenas to Santa Elena, 2 p.m.).

Cows and egrets in Monteverde pasture.

The reserve, partially donated by the Quakers, covers the upper slopes of the continental divide and laps over to the upper slopes on the east side. It has definite wet and dry seasons, though the upper levels have fog or rain much of the year. Paths wind for miles through the reserve which you can enter for a small fee that helps pay maintenance. There's more here than you can see in a day, even if you rent a horse. Many rare species, including the quetzal and the golden toad, are here among the several forest zones. You can come on a nature tour or on your own. There are several hotels and pensions as well as rooms for rent by local people if you're staying longer and living simply. You should have reservations here, as all hotels are sometimes full. While there is camping allowed, you'd be damp and cold rather soon.

Light rain gear or Goretex, and polyester bunting clothes that dry quickly are welcome. You'll want an umbrella in your day pack, which should be waterproof if you're going to walk far. Hiking boots are a must though they can be light. You'll want lightweight field glasses and a bird book. You can get bird and animal checklists as well as trail maps here. You'll see more in

Monteverde child feeds his baby goat.

less time with a guide on a nature tour, but quiet walking on your own is a memorable experience and the local people are friendly and helpful. Locally there are guides available and horses for rent.

Note that while November through January is best for hummingbirds and amphibians, it's easier to see quetzals, three-wattled bellbirds, and possibly the bare-necked umbrella bird in March and April when they're mating and nesting, too busy to be as cautious as usual.

The Monteverde Conservation League, made up mostly of local people, is raising funds to buy additional land needed for habitat. If you're interested, please read our chapter, So You'd Like to Help, later in this book.

Recently a road has been opened to Tilarán from Santa Elena so it is possible to make a circuit instead of simply going up and back on the main road.

Where To Stay

Hotel de Montaña Monteverde: First class hotel with 12 modern rooms overlooking the Gulf of Nicoya in the distance. Box lunches, guides and rental horses available. Will pick up guests from bus in Santa Elena. Reader reports vary. Tours from San Jose can include day on Calypso yacht in gulf.

Hotel Belmar at Monteverde.

Belmar: Very attractive chalet style with balconies, fine view, large rooms, woods close by. Hospitable staff. Recommended.

Pension Quetzal: Very attractive modern pension with pleasant rooms, beautiful wood. Friendly place. Bird bath at edge of woods attracts many and provides a good photo spot. Biologists often stay here. Rate includes 3 meals and box lunch is available when needed. Recommended.

	La Ronda (Liberia)	La Siesta (Liberia)	Oriental (Liberia)	Hacienda La Pacifica (Cañas)	Cabinas El Sueño (Tilarán)	Cabinas Mary (Tilarán)	Cabinas Naralit (Tilarán)	Central (Tilarán)	De la Montaña Monteverde	Belmar (Monteverde)	Pension Quetzal	Flor Mar
Price Range	F	F	F	D	F	F	F	F	C	C	D	E
Cleanliness	very good	exc	good	exc	exc	exc	exc	very good	exc		exc	exc
Noise Level	exc	exc	varies	exc	exc	very good	exc	exc	exc		exc	exc
English Spoken				x					x	x	x	x
Pool	x	x		x								
On Waterfrnt												
Tv												
Elevator												
Bar	x	x	x	x	x		x		x	x		
Restaur't	x	x	x	x	x		x		x	x	x	x
Parking	x	x		x	x	x	x	x	x	x	x	x
Air Cond Or Fan	x	x	x	x								
Courtesy Transp.												
In Town		x	x		x	x	x	x				
W/Bath	all	all	all	all	all	4	all	8	all	all	2	2
Rooms No. Of	25	25	28	23	20	6	16	19	15	9	8	10
Telephone	66-04-17	66-06-78	66-00-85	69-00-50		69-54-70	69-53-93	69-53-63	61-18-46	61-10-01	61-09-01	61-09-01
Address	S. on I-A Hwy, Apdo. 91, Liberia	Apdo. 15, Liberia	Ave. 2, I-A Hwy, Ave. 1, Calle 12, Liberia	4 km N. Cañas, Cañas	Tilarán	Frente del Parque, Tilarán	Tilarán	Tilarán	Apdo. 70, Plaza Gonzales Visques, San Jose, CR	Monteverde	Apdo. 10165, San Jose, CR	Apdo. 10165, San Jose, CR

Price ranges for single room: A+, over $70; A, $54-70; B, $36-54; C, $24-36; D, $14-24; E, $8-14; F, up to $8. Plus 13% tax.

Pension Flor Mar: Basic, but pleasant, friendly. Price includes 3 meals. Can get box lunch. Rooms have bunk beds for 3 or 4. Nearest to reserve, 1½ km. Camping area adjacent.

Taxi from Santa Elena to pensions is about $6 each way.

Pension Santa Elena: In village of Santa Elena, near bus, but miles from reserve. Basic, not inspected. Reported noisy on weekends.

This pasture on the road to Monteverde was forest 40 years ago.

North and South Central

These separate areas, the "everywhere else" after we've discussed the areas with major tourist attractions, are getting only brief mention in this edition for several reasons. They are interesting and sometimes beautiful places, but they can't compete with the coasts or the Meseta Central for the first time visitor's limited time. Except for the Inter-American Highway running through the Valle General, roads are often poor or non-existent. Most hotels are basic, well below the level most foreign travelers want. Finally, the political and military situation in Nicaragua has led to tension along the northern border, especially in its

Hundred year-old farm worker's cabin of hand-hewn timbers.

High-stepping criollo horse prances into village.

long central section, which is rugged and not easily patrolled. I hope with everyone else that these conditions improve and our next edition can explore these area in detail while encouraging personal driving to Costa Rica.

For our purpose, south central refers to the Talamanca Mountains south of Chirripó and the Valles de General and Coto Brus. From the east, you can ride buses from Puerto Limón To Bribri near the base of these mountains. From there into the Indian reserves or up into the mountains requires 4-wheel drive until roads run out entirely and you're on foot. Especially in wet season, even the locals have trouble getting around. Several thousand Indians, remnants of pre-Columbian tribes, live in reserves granted by the government on the eastern slopes of the Talamancas. These bound the national parks of Chirripó and La Amistad.

On the west side, the Valles de General and Coto Brus are a developing farming area with a variety of traditional and new crops. The Inter-American Highway drops (often suddenly in the wet season or during earthquakes!) from the mountains down to San Isidro, the largest town and governmental center. Accommodations here are good to basic and reasonably priced.

Del Sur: Very attractive hotel a few miles south of town with big pool. During semana santa I found many Costa Rican families from San Jose here, enjoying themselves and avoiding crowds at the beach! Excellent value. Recommended.

From San Isidro you can take buses to Playa Dominical on the coast or up Chirripó National Park headquarters on the edge of San Gerardo de Rivas. The Inter-American highway continues down the valley, down the river to Palmar and on to the Panamanian border. Buses to the border are crowded in the weeks before Christmas as Costa Ricans ride down from San Jose to shop in stores just over the border. Near Palmar the basaltic spheres of all sizes carved by prehistoric peoples are found.

In this area Costa Ricans and foreigners are developing fincas usually well off the main road. If you make their acquaintance and can visit, you will see pioneer life in the modern tropics and possibly some wildlife.

To reach La Amistad National Park, you can take a bus to San Vito from San Jose and then over a very rugged road 30 km. to Las Mellizas. You should discuss this with the park authorities in San Jose first as you need permission and should get advice on routes from Las Mellizas, as well as what to bring.

To reach Las Cruces, or the Wilson Botanical Gardens, maintained by the Organization For Tropical Studies, take the San Vito bus from San Jose, a 6 hour ride. You can then take another bus or taxi the last 6 km. The gardens fill 30 acres, buffered by another 270 acres of forest reserve, with miles of trails, and one of the world's finest collections of bromeliads and other tropical plants. This isn't a place to rush through, and you can arrange in advance with the OTS office in San Jose to stay in their dormitory. Ask if you can eat with them, or bring our own food.

A pair of boxwood dancers at Zarcero.

224

North central refers to the area east and north of the volcano chain including the Cordilleras de Guanacaste, Tilarán, and Central. It's a rolling to hilly area that flattens out to the Caribbean lowland on the east. Roads lead from the Meseta Central to this region via Sarchí to Ciudad Quesada and via Heredia to Puerto Viejo on the beautiful Sarapiqui River (there are lots of Puerto Viejos in Costa Rica!). There are buses to both towns. At Ciudad Quesada, the largest town for some distance in the region, a cooperative has recently opened a store selling local arts and crafts. The road to Puerto Viejo passes 2 of Costa Rica's finest waterfalls and offers a great view over the northern region.

La Selva Biological Reserve, near Puerto Viejo, adjoins Braulio Carrillo National Park, providing a continuous strip of natural habitat from the lowland to the top of Barva Volcano. La Selva is operated by the Organization for Tropical Studies (address in our Sources section) involving several universities. It's a place for studying natural lowland rainforest, but has nature trails which you can walk and even rustic quarters at the reserve where you can stay. The charge is higher for tourists to help support research in the reserve ($12 for lunch, trails and guide per day, or $70 for room, board and guide). Some international nature tours offer a trip of La Selva. There are basic hotels in Puerto Viejo and 2 nearby private lodges with their own forest reserves on which they lead tours:

Rara Avis: Rustic lodge owned by Amos Bien, former administrator of La Selva, on 1500 acres of forest. Good chance to learn this area in depth if you're ready to hike muddy trails in rainforest. Some trips include backpacking. Price covers meals, bunk, and guide.

Selva Verde Lodge: Lodge owned by Holbrook Travel in Florida on nearly 400 acres of private forest. Biologists give workshops and tours. Range C includes meals.

You may want to do a loop trip through part of the north central plain, driving or riding a bus from Tilarán around Lake Arenal through Fortuna to Ciudad Quesada and back via Zarcero and Sarchí to San José. It's the scenic route back from Guanacaste and a great contrast to the dryness there.

Sarchí artist puts finishing touches on a traditionally painted oxcart wheel.

You'll be driving around the north end of Lake Arenal, passing first the pump station that sends water west to Guanacaste and then the dam that forms the lake and keeps the water from flowing to the Caribbean. In between is the only bad road of the whole trip, about 10 km of mud and potholes—OK for 2-wheel drive if you take it slowly. Shortly you drive through some beautiful multi-story rainforest near the lake that makes it all worthwhile.

At Tabacón, about 4 km beyond the lake, you can enjoy hot spring water from the Volcano Arenal in pools for soaking. Anywhere you stop along the highway you'll hear an occasional rumble from the volcano, and if you're there at night, you can see bright ash and rock thrown up in the air—if it's one of the mountain's active periods as 1987 was.

In Fortuna, **Hotel Central**, facing the park, wasn't inspected but looked OK. It's on the corner, second floor. Every town must have a Hotel Central. In Ciudad Quesada **La Central** is a big new hotel with simple rooms, a good choice for overnight though not deluxe.

While some maps show a straight highway south to the Inter-American Hwy., it hasn't been built, and you will have a winding road with many trucks from Ciudad Quesada back through Zarcero and Sarchí to the main road. This traffic may be better on weekends than mid-week. Don't let it stop you from exploring Costa Rica!

	Del Sur (SOUTH CENTRAL)	Rara Avis (NORTH CENTRAL)	Selva Verde Lodge	La Central
Price Range	E	C	C	F
Cleanliness	very good	exc	exc	good
Noise Level	exc	exc	exc	high
English Spoken		x	x	
Pool	x			
On Waterfrnt				
Tv				
Elevator				
Bar	x			
Restaur't	x		x	
Parking	x	x	x	
Air Cond Or Fan	x		x	
Courtesy Transp.				
In Town				
W/Bath	all		4	all
Rooms No. Of	60	4	11	50
Telephone	71-02-33	53-08-44	71-64-59	46-03-01
Address	5 km S. San Isidro Apdo. 4 San Isidro	Puerto Viejo Apdo. 8105 1000 San Jose	Chilamate Puerto Viejo Sarapiqui	Quesada San Carlos, CR

Price ranges for single room: A+, over $70; A, $54-70; B, $36-54; C, $24-36; D, $14-24; E, $8-14; F, up to $8. Plus 13% tax.

Tortuguero Nat'l. Park headquarters.

NATIONAL PARKS

You've already heard of the significance of Costa Rica's park system. Here's a brief outline of the attractions of individual parks and how you can visit. If you're not on a guided tour and are going to see more than Irazú, Poás, Braulio Carrillo, and Manuel Antonio, which are heavily used and organized to handle crowds, you need to stop in at Park Service headquarters, Ave. 9, Calle 17/19, San Jose. Tel. 23-23-98.

Permission is required to visit most other parks and all the biological reserves, which are preserved in unaltered condition for research purposes. Park headquarters has a 24 hour radio net with the parks, often their only way of getting assistance in an emergency. At headquarters there are bilingual staff who can get you the latest info on roads and conditions in the park. Out at the parks, Spanish may be the only language. Staff at the parks is so limited that they must know when to expect visitors and whether you will need meals, camping areas or bunkrooms (if they have them), guides, information, or horses (which may be available at reasonable cost, but only if the park can spare them and tack, and only by prior arrangement). This is your best chance to find out what to bring and what to expect.

The Park Service has a very useful guide to the parks with the significance of each and some of the facilities (though more have been added since). It has bus info for reaching the parks. You'll soon note that most of the buses getting closest to the remote parks go to villages that aren't on any map you can find and let you off 10 or 15 km. from the park entrance (not what you may be used to)! Maps and wildlife checklists may be bought at the CIDA office in the National Zoo in San Jose. In many cases the nearest food is sold 20 or more miles from the park. Topographic maps are available at bookstores or the National Geographic Institute near Plaza Viquez, east of the Pacific Railroad station.

Costa Rica's national parks need and depend on international support as they've only been established a few years and the country has been unable to build needed facilities or, more inportant, to buy all the private land within them—in some cases a large proportion of the park. Information on where and how you can help is given in the "So You'd Like to Help" chapter.

Dimensions of the parks are given in hectares, equal to 2.5 acres. Parks we haven't discussed in detail include:

Tortuguero: This is the green turtle nesting site you've probably seen on TV. July through September is the peak nesting season, with hatching two months later. The park has nature trails as well as river channels you can explore by boat to see many land and sea birds, monkeys, and even the rare manatee. Several tour agencies come here, and Costa Rica Expeditions runs some tours to Tortuga Lodge on which you fly one way, using the strip. Park headquarters at the south end of the village and the Green Turtle Research Station started by Archie Carr, about a mile north, are worth visiting. Note that government boat from Moin gives priority to locals needing transport, so room isn't always available to tourists. There are two tipico restaurants in the village, both good. You may be able to rent a dugout to do your own exploring, or hire a local guide with a boat if you're traveling independently. Beach walking is fun even by day to see turtle tracks from the night before as well as what washed up.

Howler monkey leaps from one tree to the next at Tortuguero.

Guayabo National Monument: 19 km. north of Turrialba on gravel road. Archeological site still being explored, once a settlement of 10,000 occupied from 1000 A.D. to 1400 A.D. Besides the ruins, there's a trail down to the Guayabo River with great birdwatching. Altitude 3,000-6,000 ft. November through March are best. From Turrialba (reached by hourly bus from San Jose), there's a bus at noon on Wednesday and Saturday and a bus at 3 p.m. on Monday and Friday.

Braulio Carrillo: On road from San Jose to Guápiles, starting 12 km from San Jose. Wildlife, several forest zones stretching from the eastern lowlands to the top of Barva Volcano. Orchids. The eastern slope has rain and clouds much of the year.

Coco Island: 360 miles offshore with reputed vast pirate and Inca treasure never found, including life-size solid gold statues of the Twelve Apostles. Occasional tours available. Otherwise reachable only by chartered boat. Some species of flora & fauna are found only there. There are hundreds of waterfalls on the island. With no facilities ashore, you do have to live on the boat.

La Amistad: Huge, straddling the upper slopes of the Talamanca Mountains, adjoining a park on Panamanian side. Its establishment more than doubled size of Costa Rican park system. Newest park, with no facilities or services, and few trails. Ask the Park Service in San Jose for latest info and current road conditions to it.

Chirripó: 43,700 hectares. It includes Cerro Chirripó, 12,530 ft., the highest point in Costa Rica, and is famous for its paramo, a high, treeless zone which has frost but no snow. From San Isidro de El General there's a bus at 5 a.m. and 2 p.m. to San Gerardo de Rivas and park headquarters. The hike takes 2 or more days, using shelters on the mountain, so you don't have to carry a tent. Ask the Park Service in San Jose for current conditions.

Corcovado: 41,789 hectares, occupying most of the Osa Peninsula on Costa Rica's southwest coast. In an area ½ the size of Yosemite National Park are 285 species of birds (more than in the U.S. and Canada combined), 139 species of mammals, and 116 reptiles and amphibians! The park was threatened by placer gold miners in its rivers, but the Costa Rican government recently removed them and the park is again open. You can get to the west side and park headquarters by chartered plane, or to the east side via bus or boat to Puerto Jimenez and several days of hot hiking from there. Tours from Marenco Biological Station land by boat on the northwest corner and hike down into the park with rangers. This, or going with a group by plane is easiest. Costa Rica Expeditions leads tours from park headquarters, organized months ahead by nature tours in the U.S.

Barra Honda: Caverns 50 to 600 feet deep with beautiful limestone formations you can visit with a ranger guide. Also dry lowland forest and low vocanic cone, Barra Honda Volcano, near Gulf of Nicoya. Water and hiking trails are the only facilities nearer than town of Nicoya, 14 km. The bus from Nicoya to Santa Ana passes about 1 km from the park.

Palo Verde: The park and adjacent wildlife preserve fill the V formed by the Tempisque and Bebedero Rivers at the head of the gulf of Nicoya. During the rainy season most of the park is flooded or swampy, except for limestone ridges in the north. It's the winter or permanent home for hundreds of species of waterfowl, including the rare jabiru stork. Camping is possible at park headquarters. Access is from Bebedero which can be reached by bus from Cañas, or you can take a cab all the way to the park from Cañas. From Bebedero it is a hot hike of several hours on rice plantation roads. If you're not roughing it, you may want to go with a nature tour, or rent a car and stay in Cañas, driving out to the park. If you use the ranger's bunkroom by reservation, do bring a bug net for sleeping. During dry season birds are concentrated along the rivers, and the easiest way to see and photograph them would be from raft or boat. The park has a nature trail on a dike which gives good early morning views of birds in the surrounding swamp.

Rincon de la Vieja: Hike to summit is only advised during dry season due to visibility. One shelter en route. There's also a bunkroom at park headquarters and use of a kitchen by arrangement at headquarters in San Jose. On trails there are several lovely single campsites at lower elevations. Don't camp or even stand longer than you have to on tick-infested lawn in front of park headquarters. Wildlife and volcanic features spectacular. Bus from Liberia unpredictable in wet weather.

Spanish-style saddle in the museum at Santa Rosa.

Santa Rosa: Costa Rica's first park was established to protect the site of Costa Rica's battle with William Walker and his men that preserved the country's independence. It also includes the Playas Naranjo (a 7 mile walk each way to a beautiful beach on which leatherback turtles nest) and Nancite (several miles farther north where huge arribadas of Pacific Ridley turtles nest). The second part of the park, the Murciélago Addition included former lands of Nicaraguan dictator, Somoza, on the south shore of Bahia Santa Elena, with beautiful white sand beaches, some an easy walk from roads leading into area, much dry forest wildlife. Dec. through April best months.

In 1987 the land between the two parts was added by President Arias. It includes the former airstrip allegedly used by the CIA to supply the contras. Putting the land into a national park seems a typically Costa Rican solution to the problem! Now Dr. Daniel Janzen and others have proposed adding a belt of land leading from the existing park eastward to the top of the cordillera, providing room for species, including birds and butterflies, which migrate up and downslope during the year. The combined park would be called Guanacaste National Park. Funds are still needed to buy the land and can be donated through the agencies listed in "So You'd Like to Help". Access is easy since the Inter-American Hwy. skirts the park. You can drive into both the first two parts, or get off at the entrances from the La Cruz bus you board at Liberia.

Besides the national parks, there are the pristine biological reserves, such as Carara and Tapantí, which you can visit by permit only or with a guided nature group. Geotur and Costa Rica Expeditions run day trips to Carara, and the latter sometimes has tours to Tapantí. These quiet places with limited trails have much more wildlife than you'll see, but with guides, you can enjoy an exciting experience.

What a lot to explore! The wilderness aspects of these parks and heavy growth in most places can give you a much greater respect for short distances! But there's so much to see and marvel at, even if you sit quietly in camp and wait to see what walks, crawls, or flies past.

Poacher at Conchal digs leatherback turtle eggs laid the night before. People who eat or drink the eggs in bars provide the market that endangers sea turtles.

SO YOU'D LIKE TO HELP

Costa Rica, as a developing nation, welcomes your help if you want to contribute to its progress as well as simply enjoy it. Besides the knowledge that you have helped, this can give you a chance to meet some wonderful people you otherwise would have missed.

Costa Rica's national parks need international support as they've only been established recently and are still being increased. The nation has been unable to build needed facilities or even to buy all the private land within them—in some cases a large proportion of the park. To protect the wildlife and plants for which the parks were established, more rangers are needed, with equipment to do the job. When I visited one park, the only jeep needed repairs, there was no fuel for the patrol boat, and the only pair of binoculars had lenses too mildewed to see through. Besides out-numbering the rangers, the poachers were better equipped.

The Fundación de Parques Nacionales, Apdo. 236, 1002 San José, (Tel. 23-84-37) was established to raise money for the parks, to set priorities for its use in the park system, and to assure that donated funds are spent for that purpose. Its office is on the 2nd floor of the edificio cristal, Ave 1, Calle 1/3. Here's one use for the money you couldn't change back to dollars on leaving or as a meaningful gift you don't have to pack for nature-loving friends at home.

Tax-deductible donations can be made from within the United States specifically for the Costa Rican Parks to:

World Wildlife Fund
1255 23rd St. NW
Washington, DC 20037

The Nature Conservancy
1785 Massachusetts Ave. NW
Washington DC 20036

While Monteverde isn't a park and is run instead by the Tropical Science Center, its needs are similar. The Monteverde Conservation League, Apdo. 10165, 1000 San José, is raising funds to buy land adjacent to the present reserve on both east and west that is essential breeding habitat for the bare-necked umbrella bird and resplendent quetzal as well as the jaguar and many other species. You can get an idea how far your dollars will go from current land prices here. An acre of rainforest with stream frontage is worth about $30 while an acre of "ordinary rainforest" goes for about $18! That's all it takes to give permanent protection to the quetzal's home. The League has agreements with some farmers to buy their land, but must raise the money before the land is deforested or sold.

Waiting for the bus in Bebedero, a village near Palo Verde National Park, I asked the man beside me where the children went to school after they finished 6th grade here. "Some go to stay with relatives in Cañas and some ride the bus every day. It costs a lot of money and they have to take their lunch. The ride is an hour each way. Most of them can't go." He didn't mention school uniforms, another cost. I asked if Bebedero had a library so those who stayed home could continue to read. "No, the nearest library is in Cañas, too."

Beside me on the curb a barefoot ten year-old girl turned the pages of the first edition of this book, reading a few English words and looking at the pictures of her country. "Ah, los canales. Que linda!"

Village libraries in towns with no high schools are the only way Costa Ricans can continue education past the 6th grade if they can't afford to live elsewhere to go to school. There are presently 95 libraries outside San Jose though the country needs hundreds more. Most of them have very few books, all of which must be read in the library. Libraries are critical in a democracy where everyone votes and must understand what he's voting for. Sra. Oduber, wife of the former president, made these her concern and helped get the system as far as it is.

To be sure that funds and books could be donated for this cause and spent accordingly, I met with staff at the National Library in San Jose and learned how the donations should be directed. To donate funds or books (new or used, Spanish preferred), address

Srta. Bera Violeta Salazar Mora
Jefe Dept. Bibliotecas Públicas
Apdo. 10.008
San Jose, Costa Rica

Specify (especificar): "Para comprar de libros de las Bibliotecas Públicas."

In San Jose one can go to the National Library across from the National Park on the hill and ask for this department. Srta. Salazar says that with such specification the money will not be spent in San Jose nor will it be used to simply build more concrete somewhere. If you'd like to help democracy in Latin America, here's a personal way to do it.

Copies of the first edition of *The Costa Rica Traveler* in Costa Rica when this edition is published are being donated to these libraries. Someday I hope all villages without libraries will at least have a few shelves of library books in the school where any villager can read them.

Retired executives can help developing nations by sharing their managerial skills with International Executive Service Corps, P.O. Box 10005, Stamford, CT 06904 in the U.S. or C.E.S.O., Suite 200, 1867 Yonge Street, Toronto, Ontario, Canada M4S 1Y5 in Canada. The program is effective in Costa Rica and our readers have enjoyed participating.

SOURCES OF INFORMATION
TOUR AGENCIES

EXCAI Tours
Calle 26/28, Paseo Colón
Edificio Doble L
Apdo. 7.347, 1000 San Jose
Phone 23-01-55, 33-66-44

Blanco Travel Service
Ave. ctl., Calle 7/9
Apdo. 4.559, 1000 San Jose
Phone 22-17-92, 22-85-92

Orchid Travel
Apdo. 812-Y Griega 1011
San Jose
Phone 38-35-86

Panorama Tours
Calle 9, Ave. ctl./1
Apdo. 7.323, 1000 San Jose
Phone 33-02-33

Rio Colorado Lodge
Apdo. 5094,
1000 San Jose
Phone 32-40-63,32-86-10
Lobby of Hotel Corobici
Fishing, canal trips,
dove hunting

T.A.M
Calle 1, Ave. ctl./1
Apdo. 1.864, 1000 San Jose
Phone 23-51-11

Agencia de Viajes Atlántico
Apdo. 1078 Centro Colón
1007 San Jose
Phone 32-27-32, 32-88-88
Canales trips

Typical Tours
Ave. 4, Calle 24/26
Apdo. 842
1000 San Jose
Phone 21-31-58

Swiss Travel Service
Lobby of Hotel Corobici
Apdo. 7-1970, 1000 San Jose
Phone 31-40-55

Fiesta Tours
Ave. 1, Calle 5/7
Apdo. 8-4320, 1000 San Jose
Phone 23-34-33

Agencia de Viajes Miki
Calle 20 sur, Paseo Colón
Apdo. 328, 1007 Centro Colón
Phone 33-06-13, 21-36-81

Interviajes
Calle 3, Ave. 4 Heredia
Apdo. 296, 3000 Heredia
Phone 38-12-12
Scenic tours for Costa
Ricans and visitors

Agencia de Viajes Las Olas
Hotel Jacó Beach
Apdo. 962, 1000 San Jose
Phone 61-12-50, 32-48-11

Nature Tours and Lodges

Calypso Tours
Apdo. 6941, 1000 San Jose
Phone 33-36-17
Boat tours in Gulf of Nicoya

Finca Ob-la-di, Ob-la-da
Villa Colón, Costa Rica
Phone 49-11-79
Horseback mountain tours

Horizontes (Marenco)
Ave. 1, Calle 1/3
Apdo. 4025-1000
San Jose
Phone 21-15-94

Aqua Sport
Apdo. 100
Playas de Coco
Guanacaste
Phone 67-00-50

Papagayo Excursions
Playa Tamarindo
Carretera San Jose-Santa Cruz
Tamarindo, Guanacaste
Phone 68-06-52
Turtle nesting and estuary cruises

The Aspinalls
Apdo 1195-1250
Escazú
Phone 55-06-59
Cabins at Arenal Volcano
and on Osa Peninsula.

Geotur
Apdo. 469 Y Griega
1011 San Jose
Phone 27-58-68

Costa Rica Expeditions
Calle ctl., Ave. 3
Apdo. 6.941, 1000 San Jose
Phone 23-99-75, 23-99-76
Raft and nature tours

Rios Tropicales
Apdo. 472-1000
Pavas
Phone 31-62-96
Raft tours

Diving Safaris, Inc.
P. O. Box 425-2010 Zapote
San Jose
Phone 24-00-33

Rara Avis
Apdo. 8105-1000
San Jose
Phone 53-08-44
Rainforest, birding, rustic lodge

EMBASSIES & CONSULATES IN/NEAR SAN JOSE

Nation	Address	Telephone
Argentina	Ave. ctl., Calle 27	
Austria	Calle 2, Ave. 2	23-28-22
Belgium	Los Yoses	25-62-55
Brazil	Calle 4, Ave. ctl.	33-15-44
Britain	Paseo Colón, Calle 38/40	21-55-66
Canada	Calle 3, Ave. ctl.	23-04-46
Colombia	Ave. 5, Calle 5	21-07-25
Chile	Bo Dent	24-42-43
China	Los Yoses	24-81-80
Ecuador	Calle 1, Ave. 5	23-62-81
El Salvador	Calle 5, Ave. ctl.	22-55-36
France	Carret Curridabat	25-07-33
Germany	Ave 3, Calle 36	21-58-11
Greece	Guayabos	25-94-13
Guatemala	Calle 24/28, Ave. 1	22-89-91
Holland	Calle 1, Ave. 2	22-73-55
Honduras	Calle 2, Ave. ctl./2	22-89-91
Italy	Calle 29, Ave. 8/10	25-20-87
Japan	Rohrmoser	32-12-55
Korea	Calle 2, Ave. 2	33-10-56
Mexico	Calle 5, Ave. 1/3	22-54-96
Nicaragua	Calle 25/27, Ave. ctl.	33-44-79
Panama	San Pedro	25-34-01
Peru	Calle 4, Ave. ctl.	22-56-44
Spain	Calle 30/32, Paseo Colón	22-19-33
Switzerland	Calle 5, Ave. 3/5	21-48-29
U.S.S.R.	Curridabat	25-57-80
U.S.A.	~~Ave. 3, Calle ctl.~~ *see Flash!*	~~33-11-55~~
Uruguay	Calle 2, Ave. 1	23-25-12
Venezuela	Los Yoses	25-88-10

Call or visit in the morning, as afternoon hours vary.

COSTA RICAN CONSULATES

Canada

614 Centre A. Street N.W.
Calgary, Alberta

7 Lia Crescent Don Mills
Toronto, Ontario, Canada

1520 Alberni Street
Vancouver 5, B.C.

1155 Dorchester Blvd. W.
Suite 2902, Montreal
P. Q. Canada H3B 2L3
(514) 866-8159
(514) 866-0442

UNITED STATES—Consulates General

Jurisdiction	Address
Washington, D.C., Maryland, West Virginia, Virginia	2112 "S" Street N.W. Washington, D. C. 20008 (202) 234-2946
New York, Pennsylvania, Connecticut, Delaware, New Jersey, Massachusetts Rhode Island, Maine, Vermont, New Hampshire, Rhode Island	80 Wall Street, Suite 1117 New York, NY 10005 (212) 425-2620 (212) 425-2621
California, Oregon, Washington, Montana, Colorado, Wyoming, Idaho, Nevada, Utah, Arizona, Alaska, Hawaii	1543 W. Olympic Blvd. Los Angeles, CA 90015 (213) 484-5040
Florida, Georgia, North and South Carolina	28 W. Flagler St., Suite 540 Miami, FL 33130 (305) 377-4242 (305) 377-4243
Louisiana, Alabama, Mississippi, Tennessee, Kentucky, Arkansas	934 International Trade Mart New Orleans, LA 70130 (504) 525-5445
Texas, Oklahoma, Kansas New Mexico	11570 Cheswood Houston, TX 77072 (713) 332-5052
Illinois, Michigan, Ohio, Indiana, Wisconsin, Minnesota, Missouri, North Dakota, South Dakota, Nebraska, Iowa	8 S. Michigan Ave. Chicago, IL 60603 (312) 787-3323
Puerto Rico	Calle 32 N 327 Avenida Amrico Miranda Jardines Metropolitanos, Rio Piedras Puerto Rico, 00927

There are many local consulates in each area. For addresses contact the Consulate General for your jurisdiction.

240

RECOMMENDED READING

Guidebooks, International, with Costa Rica section:

South America on a Shoestring, by Geoff Crowther, Lonely Planet Publications, Australia. Lists hotels up to $7.00 per night. Much bus and transportation information.

The South American Handbook, Trade & Travel Publication Ltd., England (distributed in the U.S. by Rand McNally). Most information for the budget traveler.

Guidebooks, Costa Rica: *The New Key to Costa Rica*, by Beatrice Blake and Anne Becher, Editoria Texto Ltda., Costa Rica. Guidebook which emphasizes living in Costa Rica.

Costa Rican Life: *The Costa Ricans*, by Richard, Karen, and Mavis Biesanz, Prentice-Hall. Very well done social history and description of the Costa Rican people. *"What Happen"*—A Folk History of Costa Rica's Talamanca Coast, by Paula Palmer, Ecodesarrollos, Costa Rica. Oral history by black coastal residents.

Natural Science: *A Field Guide to Mexican Birds and Adjacent Central America,* by Roger Tory Peterson, Houghton-Mifflin. (Worth picking up before you leave the U.S.—it costs twice as much in Costa Rica.)

A Guide to the Birds of Panama, by Robert Ridgely, Princeton University Press. Same note as above.

Costa Rica: Country Environmental Profile—a field Study, available in bookstores or at the Tropical Science Center, San Jose. Excellent in-depth study of environmental issues in Costa Rica.

Costa Rican Natural History, edited by Daniel H. Janzen, University of Chicago Press. Thorough discussion of the geography, climate, flora, and fauna of Costa Rica.

The National Parks of Costa Rica, by Mario Boza and Rolando Mendoza, INCAFO, Spain. Study of Costa Rica's national parks with beautiful photographs.

USEFUL ADDRESSES

Instituto Costarricense de Turismo
Apdo. 777
San Jose, Costa Rica
Phone 23-17-33

ICT Office of Tourist Information
Plaza de la Cultura
Calle 5. Ave. ctl./2
Open Monday through Friday.
8:00 a.m. to 4:30 p.m.

Costa Rican Tourist Board
200 S. E. First Street, Suite 400
Miami, FL 33131
305-358-2150 or 800-327-7033
After April 1, 1987, moved to
1101 Brickell Ave.
Miami, FL 33131 (same phones)
(main office for inquiries)

Costa Rican Tourist Board
3540 Wilshire Blvd., Suite 404
Los Angeles, CA 90010
800-762-5900 or 213-382-8080

The Tico Times
P. O. Box 4632
San Jose, Costa Rica
(located: Ave. 6, Calle 13)
Phone 22-89-52, 22-00-44

Language Institutes:

INTENSA
Apdo. 8110-1000
San Jose
Phone 25-60-09, 24-63-53

ASCONA
Apdo. 83790
1000 San Jose
Costa Rica
Phone 33-31-88
(conservation association)

North American-Costa Rican
 Cultural Center
Apdo. 1489
San Jose
Phone 25-94-33

TICA Bus
Calle 9, Ave. 4 San Jose
Phone 21-89-54

Instituto Internacional Forester
75 m south of Automercado Los Yoses
San Jose
Phone 25-16-49

National Park Service
Ave. 9, Calle 17/19
San Jose, Costa Rica
Phone 33-52-84, 33-56-73

Instituto Universal de Idioma
Apdo. 164
San Jose, Costa Rica
Phone 23-96-62

Fundacion de Parques Nacionales
Apdo. 236
1002 San Jose, Costa Rica
Phone 22-49-21, 23-84-37

Conversa
Apdo. 17 Centro Colón
San Jose, Costa Rica
Phone 21-76-49, 33-24-18

Tropical Science Center
Calle 1, Ave. 2
(2 blks s. of Metr. Cathedral)
San Jose, Costa Rica
Phone 22-62-41

American Institute for
 Language & Culture
Apdo. 200
1001 San Jose, Costa Rica
Phone 25-43-13

World Wildlife Fund
1601 Connecticut Ave.
Washington, D. C. 20009
(202) 387-0800

The Nature Conservancy
International Program
1785 Massachusetts Ave.
N. W. Washington, D. C. 20036
(703) 841-5300

USEFUL WORDS AND PHRASES

abanico = fan
abierto = open
agua = water
agua caliente = hot water
aire (con, sin) = air
  conditioning
alto = stop
Apartado(Apdo.) = post office
  box
apartotel = apartment hotel
almuerzo = lunch
alto = high
amable = kind
aquí = here
arroz = rice
avenida = avenue
ayer = yesterday
azúcar = sugar
azul = blue

bajo = low
baño (con, sin) = bath
barato = cheap
blanco = white
bolsa = bag
bueno = good
buenos días = hello

cabina = cabin
café = coffee
cafe negro=black coffee
calle = street
cambio = change (money)
carne = meat
caro = expensive
casado = basic meal
cena = supper
cerrado = closed
cerveza = beer
claro = light
comer = eat
comida = meal, dinner
comprar = to buy

con leche = coffee with
  cream
correo = post office
cuarto = room
cuarto silencio = quiet room
cuenta = restaurant or hotel
  check

derecha = right
desayuno = breakfast
deseo = I want
dificil = difficult
dolor = pain
domingo = Sunday
dónde está = where is

ensalada = salad
entrada = entrance
escuela = school
esta noche = tonight
estacion, no estacion = parking
estampillas = stamps
este = east
fácil = easy
farmacia = drug store
finca = ranch
frijoles = beans
frito = fried

gerente = manager
gracias = thank you
grande = big, large
gris = gray

habla inglés = do you speak
  English?
hable usted más despacio, por
  favor = please speak
  more slowly.
hasta luego (adiós) = goodbye

243

hay, no hay = there is, there
  isn't
helado = ice cream
hermosa = beautiful
hoy = today
huevo = egg

iglesia = church
impuesto = tax (e.g., on hotel
  bills)
izquierda = left

jamón = ham
jueves = Thursday

leche = milk
lechuga = lettuce
llave = key
lado = side
limpio = clean
lluvia = rain
lunes = Monday

malo = bad
mañana = tomorrow, morning
martes = Tuesday
médico = doctor
mercado = market
mi cuenta, por favor = I wish my
  bill please
miércoles = Wednesday
muy = very

naranjo = orange
negro = black
noche = night
norte = north

oeste = west
oficina = office
oscuro = dark

pan = bread
paragua = umbrella (man's)
pension = inexpensive hotel,
  but does not indicate that
  meals are served
papas = potatoes
pequeño = small

pescado = sh
pimoenta = pepper
piña = pineapple
piscina = swimming pool
playa = beach
poco = little
pollo = chicken
por favor = please
pulpería = small grocery store

que = what, who
Qué hora es? = What time is it?
queso = cheese
quiere usted = do you want
que quiere usted? = what do
  you want?
quiero = I want, I wish

rápido = fast
recto = straight ahead
rojo = red

sábado = Saturday
sal = salt
salida = exit
semana = week
sucio = dirty
sud = south

tarde = late, afternoon
temprano = early
tico (tica, female) = Costa
  Rican term for themselves
tiene = you, he, she, have or
  has
tostadas = toast
tipico = typical

ventana = window
verde = green
viernes = Friday

Numbers

uno = 1
dos = 2
tres = 3
cuatro = 4
cinco = 5
seis = 6
siete = 7
ocho = 8
nueve = 9
diez = 10
once = 11
doce = 12
trece = 13
quatorce = 14
quince = 15
diez y seis = 16
diez y siete = 17

diez y ocho = 18
diez y nueve = 19
veinte = 20
veintiuno = 21
veintidos = 22
treinta = 30
cuarenta = 40
cincuenta = 50
sesenta = 60
setenta = 70
ochenta = 80
noventa = 90
cien = 100
doscientos = 200
trescientos = 300
cuatrocientos = 400
quinientos = 500

seiscientos = 600
setecientos = 700
ochocientos = 800
novecientos = 900
mil = 1000
dos mil = 2000

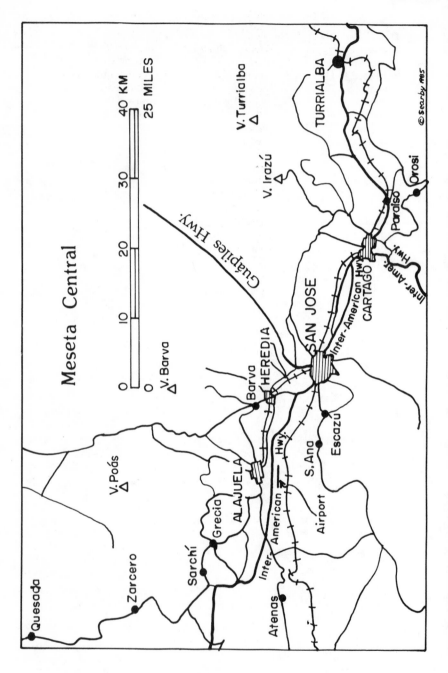

Ellen Searby holds jaguar cub born in Parque Bolivar Zoo.

Ellen Searby has traveled in 38 countries and 47 of the United States by jet, her own 2-seat plane, car, bicycle, canoe, raft, and on foot. She earned a B.A. in biology and an M.A. in geography from Stanford. She lived in Alaska and worked on the Alaska ferries from 1975 to 1990, first as a Forest Service naturalist answering thousands of travelers' questions, and then as a member of the crew. Using her knowledge of travelers' needs and concerns, she writes and publishes *Alaska's Inside Passage Traveler*, an annually updated guide to Alaska's ferries and the Inside Passage.

When she came to Costa Rica on a much-needed vacation, people who saw her Alaska book persuaded her to write one for Costa Rican visitors, clearly explaining the choices they would have in sights, activities and facilities. She returned to do the research, and the result is *The Costa Rica Traveler*. She continues her research and photography in Costa Rica, enoying Costa Rican friendliness with her combined work and play.

Ellen Searby is married to retired forestry pilot, Henry Jori. In spring 1990 she retired from the Alaska ferry to full-time writing and publishing, now living on the family farm in northern California redwoods.

Index

Index

NOTES

FLASH!

SANSA, the internal airline of Costa Rica flies 6 days a week to Quepos, Golfito, and Coto 47, and several times weekly to Playa Tamarindo, Nosara, Sámara and Palmar Sur on the west coast and to Barra Colorado on the Caribbean side, saving time and energy getting to those resorts. Adult fares range from US$15 to $35 one way.

American Airlines, (800) 433-7300, now flies from Miami to Costa Rica daily. It is expected to replace **Eastern** on its Latin American routes soon.

The exchange rate is increasing every few weeks with mini-devaluations of the colon against the dollar. For your convenience, here's a short conversion table at 90 colones per US dollar, which the colon will reach in 1990.

$ 1=	90 colones	10 colones=	$ .11
5=	450 "	20 " =	.22
10=	900 "	50 " =	.55
20=	1800 "	100 " =	1.11
100=	9000 "	500 " =	5.56
		1000 " =	11.11

Readers have noted that the hotel tax of 13% and the combined tax and service charge in restaurants of 20% add substantially to your final bill and should be allowed for.

Hotels in San Jose during high tourist season (December through April) and at the beach on holidays are frequently full. You should make reservations. Some require a deposit to hold bookings. While more hotels are being built, some in popular areas have raised their prices recently. Using the same price ranges we used throughout the book, here are the high season single ranges for many tourist hotels without taxes in 1990:

Range A+, over $70--Guanamar, Cariari, Corobici, Flamingo, La Selva O.T.S. (includes meals), Marenco (meals), Mariposa (breakfast & dinner), Rara Avis (meals), Sheraton Herradura, Tiskita Lodge (meals). **Range A,** $54-70--Arenal Observatory (meals included), Condovac La Costa, Irazu, El Ocotal, Tamarindo, Tortuga Lodge, Villagio. **Range B,**$36-54--Balmoral, Bougainvillea, Brisas Del Pacifico, Quetzal, Las Cruces (includes meals), Divisamar, Drake's Bay Wilderness (meals), Europa, Flor De Itabo, Gran Hotel Costa Rica, La Hacienda, Los Inocentes (meals), Nosara, La Pacifica (meals), Palo Verde O.T.S. (meals), Portobello, Presidente, Selva Verde (meals), C. R. Tennis Club, Torremolinos. **Range C,** $24-36--Ambassador, Amstel, La Arboleda, Belmar, Las Espuelas, Heliconia, Jungle Lodge, Montaña Monteverde, Flor Mar. **Range D,** $14-24--Acon, Del Sur, Las Olas, Tioga.

New San Jose hotels include: **L'Ambiance**, Range A+ including breakfast, luxurious. 7 rooms. C 13, Av 9/11. Apdo. 1040-2050 San Jose. Phone 22-67-02, 23-15-98, **Cacts**, Range E including continental breakfast, plain but hospitable and secure in good neighborhood. Very good value in budget hotel. C 28/30, Av 3. Apdo. 379-1005 San Jose. Phone 21-29-28, **D'Galah**, Range D, std. rooms and kitchenettes, music room with organ. North side of University of Costa Rica. Excellent value. Apdo. 85-2350 San Jose. Phone 34-17-43, 53-75-39. Nearby is **Bougainvillea/ Santo Domingo**, Range B, under same ownership as the Bougainvillea in San Jose. Resort hotel on mountainside 10 minutes from downtown. Very popular. All rooms have 2 queen beds and balconies. Apdo. 69-2120, San Jose. 40-66-22.

In Escazú, **Aparthotel Maria Alexandra**, Range C. Has pool, wheelchair accessible. Monthly rates. Av 23, C 3 in Escazú. Apdo. 3756-1000, San Jose. Phone 28-15-07.

North of Limón, on the road to Portete is the **Maribu Caribe**, Range A. Resort hotel on hill above beach, with pool. Apdo. 623-7300, Limón. 58-45-43, and 58-40-10.

For the best news we've had in years, see our immigration section starting on page 69. With a passport U.S. and Canadian citizens (and many others) can enter Costa Rica for up to 90 days without needing extensions or exit visas. Without a passport, but with proof of citizenship in two forms, you can get a tourist card good for 30 days. The law was changed in 1989. Retirees planning to move to Costa Rica as pensionados should note that a minimum pension of $600 per month is required. At the Pensionado Office in ICT you fill out the form for Seguridad, the security ministry, and wait for its return from Interpol before applying with the remainder of the required forms. Pensionados living in Costa Rica reemphasize that you should spend some time in the country and talk with those who live here before making a permanent move. The legislative assembly has made several recent changes in the law that have caused some to leave Costa Rica. New pensionado brochures are available, in Spanish.

Nature travel in Costa Rica continues to grow, with rustic nature lodges popping up in remote spots all over the country. Some save considerable areas of rainforest around them. If you're looking for rare birds or a large number of species, you'll want to pick a lodge that's contiguous with a national park rather than being an island of trees surrounded by farmland. For example, **Rara Avis**, adjacent to Braulio Carrillo Park has catalogued 330 species of birds and they're still counting!

Roads to some of these are primitive to non-existent, especially in the rainy season. Except that there really isn't a very dry season any time in a rain forest. You should definitely bring good rain gear (rubber boots are cheap in San Jose in sizes lower than 12. Bring your own in larger sizes.) A reader recommends nylon gaiters to keep pants dry and protect from mud, snakes and chiggers.

Most important is to use whatever transportation the lodge offers, and regard *getting there* as part of the experience. While you can rent 4-wheel drive vehicles, only the locals know where the shallow spot is in the river you have to drive across or where the latest holes are between the 2 mud-covered logs they call a bridge. In our Nature Tours & Lodges list on page 238 you'll find **Rara Avis, Marenco**, the **Aspinalls** who own **Arenal Observatory** and **Tiskita** on the Osa Peninsula, and others.

Drake's Bay Wilderness Camp, Range A, offers packages for at least 2 people including meals, guides and horses to Corcovado Park (can camp overnight in park), boat to Caño Island. c/o Explore Costa Rica, Apdo. 98-8150, Pavas, San Jose. Phone 71-24-36, 20-21-21. **El Gavilan Lodge**, Range A, offers packages to the Sarapiqui River, down the river by boat through fine wildlife viewing. Apdo. 445-2010, Zapote, San Jose. Phone 53-6540. In Rincón de la Vieja Nat'l. Park, **Hacienda Guachipelín**, Range A, offers tours on horseback through the park and to the volcano's summit. Apdo. 114, Liberia, Guanacaste. Phone 66-04-73.

Monteverde is very popular, and while additional hotels are planned, you should be sure you have reservations, especially during the dry season. There is now direct bus service from the Mi Bus stop near the Coca Cola station in San Jose, leaving Monday, Tuesday and Thursday at 2:30 p.m. and Saturday at 6:30 a.m. From Monteverde it leaves the cheese factory on Friday and Sunday at 3 p.m. and on Tuesday and Thursday at 6:30 a.m. The ride takes about 4.5 hours. Fare is about 250 colones one way.

Costa Rica Natural History Tours is a new tour operator. Luis Murillo, Apdo. 296-3000, Heredia, Costa Rica. Phone 38-12-12 or 33-44-57. Mario Boza, one of the founders of the national park system, is its advisor.

At Tortuguero the owners of **"Miss Caribe"** tour boat have built the comfortable Jungle Lodge.

Rios Tropicales is offering sea kayaking trips for beginners to advanced kayakers, featuring the islands and wildlife of the Gulf of Nicoya.

Cahuita and the southeast coast of Costa Rica are much more accessible now with the Guápiles Highway offering a spectacular view of Braulio Carrillo Park cloud forest on the way to Puerto Limón and then a paved road south. An express bus (the Sixaola bus) leaves San Jose at 6 a.m. and 2 p.m. daily, making the run in 3 hours and 20 minutes. The morning run gets you there in time to enjoy the day and see the whole route in daylight.

Cahuita is growing, but is still quiet on weekdays and has lowered the decibel level on the cantinas! Several new sets of cabinas, two small hotels, and **Cahuita Tours** (glass-bottomed boat tours of reef and land tours back into the Talamanca Indian Reserve) serve the visitor. **Restaurant Edith** serves great Caribbean cooking, including a vegetarian menu, lobster, and on weekends, homemade ice cream with tropical fruit.

Puerto Viejo has two sets of attractive rooms, one owned by Stanford Brown who has the seafood restaurant and the other by Vincente Guthrie. Both men are a privilege to meet. Unfortunately the only village phone at present, 58-38-44, won't always relay messages to them for reservations. Best is to call the number and ask to have either of the men call you back--without mentioning rooms.

In the Gulf of Nicoya, Isla Jesusita resort is permanently closed.

Unleaded gas isn't available in Costa Rica, though the government refinery is considering producing it.

The new U.S. embassy is in the suburb of Pavas, west of San Jose. Apdo. 10053, San Jose. Phone 203939. The Pavas bus leaves from the south side of the Coca Cola, Av 1, C 16. The A.I.D. (Agency for International Develop-ment) building is adjacent to the embassy.

The new serpentarium in San Jose features Costa Rican snakes and frogs and is probably the only place you'll see them in the country. If you want to see the fer-de-lance, bushmaster, and coral snake up close, safely, this is your spot. It also has snakes from other areas including a 19 foot Asian python. Av 1, C 9/11. Phone 55-42-10. Open seven days a week, 10 a.m.-7 p.m. Admission US$1. Feeding is Thursday morning before opening, but you can call ahead for an appointment.

Birds of Costa Rica by Stiles and Skutch is published! Cornell University Press, 124 Roberts Place, Ithaca, NY 14850-2426. (607) 257-7000. 656 pages. $65 hb. $35 pap. (You didn't want the weight anyway.) They take credit cards. Some travel stores have it.

I would appreciate any comments or information you're willing to pass along after your trip. Many of you have been very helpful, with corrections and changes as well as with your experiences as hotels and tours changed management. This book is updated regularly and small useful tips can be added in this section when we reprint. I apologize for not having time to plant trips or answer questions (unless we meet in Costa Rica). Several thousand readers quickly out-number me and the 24-hour day.

Costa Rica is a wonderful place with some of the world's finest people. I hope you'll come and explore it--and have as great a time in this peaceful country as I have!

Readers of this edition who would like a **free update flyer** after 6/1/90, are welcome to write Windham Bay Press, Box 1198, Occidental, CA 95465 and request it.

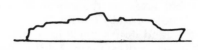

Books from Windham Bay Press, for the independent traveler:

Alaska's Inside Passage Traveler, See More/Spend Less, 13th edition by Ellen Searby. Photos, maps, 208 pages. Tells all you need to know to plan any trip you want in the Inside Passage. This handy guide explains how to make the most of the Alaska ferry system, lists all facilities in Southeast Alaska and Prince Rupert, B.C. with their prices, from deluxe hotels to cabins and youth hostels. Easy to read and use, with no paid advertising to weigh down your purse or pack. Enjoy a vacation according to your special interests on this beautiful coast. $10.95. ISBN 0-942297-03-2

The Costa Rica Traveler, Getting Around in Costa Rica, 2nd edition, by Ellen Searby. Photos, maps, 256 pages. Peace, beauty, freedom. Enjoy this tropical Camelot with its friendly people, miles of uncrowded beaches, tropical rain forest, volcanoes, and jungle waterways. See the country that has 1/10th of the world's bird species, over 1200 species of orchids, altitudes from the Atlantic and Pacific Oceans to 12,600 feet, all in an area the size of West Virginia! Here is some of the world's best deep-sea fishing, snorkeling, river rafting--all at reasonable cost. We inspected over 200 hotels and update at each printing. Hotels, transportation, and sights are clearly described so you can choose well. $11.95. ISBN 0-9605526-9-3.

Vancouver Island Traveler, Great Adventures on Canada's West Rim, by Sandy Bryson. Waters teeming with fish and whales, world-class diving and skiing, mild winters with green forests and lush golf courses at the seashore, kayaking a wild west coast, board sailing fresh lake winds, bicycling into sunsets over Victoria harbor--where is all this water adventure with friendly people, easy to reach but still a priceless treasure? Canada's Vancouver Island, just a short ferry or plane ride west of Seattle and Vancouver. *Vancouver Island Traveler* gives you all the information you need to plan an exciting or relaxing getaway trip doing what you like to do best. *Vancouver Island Traveler* takes you there! Photos, maps, 208 pages. $10.95. ISBN 0-942297-00-8.

Travelers, See More, Spend Less!

These books are at your travel bookstore, or order from Windham Bay Press. Box 1198, Occidental, CA 95465   Have a wonderful trip!

Windham Bay Press, Box 1198, Occidental, CA 95465

Number		Price	Amount
_____	*Alaska's Inside Passage Traveler*	$10.95	_____
_____	*Costa Rica Traveler*	$11.95	_____
_____	*Vancouver Island Traveler*	$10.95	_____

Postage and Handling: All prices in US $ only.   _____
(US surface $1 first book, .50 ea. add'l. Air, $2.50 first book, .50 ea. add'l.
Canada surface $1.50 first, $1 ea. add'l. Air, $3 first book, $1 ea. add'l.
Europe, Asia, Air $6.50 first book, $5 ea. add'l.)

Please add 6% Calif. sales tax for orders shipped to Calif. addresses $_____
Total Payment Enclosed $_____
Name_____
Address_____
City_____State/Prov._____
Zip_____Country_____